MW00824339

THE
IMAGE
DOCTOR

LIFESUCCESS PUBLISHING, LLC
8900 E Pinnacle Peak Road, Suite D240
Scottsdale, AZ 85255
Telephone: 800.473.7134
Fax: 480.661.1014
E-mail: admin@lifesuccesspublishing.com

ISBN   (hardcover)   978-1-59930-261-4
ISBN   (e-book)   978-1-59930-262-1

Cover : Derek Brigham
Cover Photography: Dianne Towalski
Layout: Fiona Dempsey & LifeSuccess Publishing

COMPANIES, ORGANIZATIONS,
INSTITUTIONS, AND INDUSTRY PUBLICATIONS:
Quantity discounts are available on bulk purchases of this book for reselling,
educational purposes, subscription incentives, gifts,
sponsorship, or fundraising. Special books or book excerpts can also
be created to fit specific needs such as private labeling with your logo
on the cover and a message from a VIP printed inside.
FOR MORE INFORMATION PLEASE CONTACT OUR
SPECIAL SALES DEPARTMENT AT
LIFESUCCESS PUBLISHING.

PRINTED IN CANADA

THE
IMAGE
DOCTOR

*Introducing the
incredibly simple*

ORANGECARD

*The ultimate tool
for love, health,
career, and
financial success!*

DR. TORY M. ROBSON

ACKNOWLEDGEMENTS

A deeply felt thank you to those who have shown the generosity of spirit to share, teach, and educate me. Without you I never would have been able to help the thousands of people who have trusted, and continue to trust me, with their health and personal development.

Of course to my mom Karri, dad Bruce, uncle Gary, sisters Tawn and Tina, and the rest of my family for their care, encouragement, and endless great memories growing up in Montana.

To Dr. Robert Larson, whose vision for me when I was a 'know it all' college kid permanently changed the direction of my life and put me on the road to professional success, I am eternally grateful.

To my future wife (who has no idea what she is in for) and lastly to God almighty for giving us all the breath and ability to leave people better than when we found them.

CONTENTS

FOREWORD

It has been my experience that few people realize the richness that is available in their lives if they would only look for it. Many people trudge through their days in shades of gray, wandering from one boring moment to another. Any color in their lives is vicarious, often experienced by watching or reading about other people who are actually enjoying life.

Tory Robson is one of those people who enjoys life. Dynamic, energetic and charismatic, he manages somehow to squeeze the most out of each moment. What's more, he manages to do the same for those people around him. Being around Tory is like being hooked up to the world's largest battery.

With *The Image Doctor*, Tory Robson has provided readers with the strategies they need to start enjoying their own lives. He has managed to communicate, in a clear and understandable way, the same energy and focus that he uses in his own life. Some naturally talented people find it difficult to teach what they know to others, yet Tory has developed strategies that anyone can put to use.

While some books focus on only one aspect of life, Tory's model is universal, encompassing love, health, career, and money. For those readers who may find their lives out of balance – their career is going great, but their love life stinks, for example – having a guide like this is truly a gift. They can simply turn to the appropriate chapter and bang! There's Tory's advice.

As readers go through the book, they will start to learn some of the reasons they make the decisions and take the actions that work against their own interests. They'll also find out more about themselves, and what is important to them. Maybe most importantly, anyone who reads this book will be better able to decide for him- or herself what they really want out of life.

For those of us lucky enough to know Tory, reading this book is like visiting with an old friend. For those of you who have not yet had the good fortune to meet him, let me assure you: this book is like having a one-on-one session with one of the brightest stars in the field of personal development. Over the past several years, Tory has been not only a resource for improving my health, but also as an inspiration in my professional life. I now am off all medications, am working out and feel younger and better than I have in years, plus I am earning Top Tier commissions at work. The "ORANGECARD" he helped me create has taken me to new levels of success I didn't think were possible. Even my mother who is 99 years old is impressed. She walks as a living example of healthy living and a positive attitude. The same that Tory is working to re-ignite in our over-stressed society.

With *The Image Doctor*, Tory Robson has provided a guide for everyone who wishes to transform their lives. Easy to use, easy to understand and applicable to a wide variety of life issues, this book should be at the top of the reading list for anyone who is ready to add color to his or her life.

Jo Harris, Businesswoman, mom, wife,
patient and friend of Dr. Robson, "The Image Doctor"

Chapter One

The Dream-Reality Gap

THE
DREAM-REALITY GAP

"If one advances confidently in the direction of his dreams, and endeavors to live the life which he has imagined, he will meet with a success unexpected in common hours."

— Henry David Thoreau

Why don't my dreams match my reality?

What's so important about first impressions?

How do I find true happiness?

Why can't I ever fulfill my expectations?

Why am I so unhappy?

I magine that you're at a wedding reception. As you enter the room, everyone turns to look at you. What do they see?

If you're a man, you may be wearing an impeccable suit, tailored to fit perfectly. Your shirt cuffs are precisely the right length, your tie is knotted perfectly, and your pant cuffs break at exactly the right point on your shoes. Your haircut is flawless, and even details such as your watch matching your belt buckle have been coordinated.

You stand tall, scan the room, and meet the eyes of every person there for just a moment before moving to the next person, letting each know that you have noticed them. Normally such eye contact would be viewed as aggressive, but you have a secret. As you survey the room, you've turned on your Power Smile.

Tiger Woods has it. So does Oprah Winfrey. That smile that lets their inner strength show—a confidence that refuses to be contained. The Power Smile isn't from a new brand of toothpaste or hours spent in the dentist chair. It comes from having confidence and knowing how to win.

The Power Smile, and everything else about the impression you make, results from knowing your purpose and striving toward it. Your outward appearance is the manifestation of inner strength. When you walk into a gathering, everything about you screams "I'm a winner!" and every person in that room knows it. Your Power Smile, and everything else about you, attracts others to you.

That first impression is important because every interaction you have with those people from now on will be based on that impression. Start off with a great impression, and you can build on it to achieve more and reach greater heights than you ever thought possible. Start off with a negative impression, and you'll spend a tremendous amount of time digging yourself out of a hole, trying to simply be at eye level with those around you.

Research shows that a first impression is generated within three seconds of meeting someone. This impression sets like concrete, so if you are serious about your success, then you must be serious about making great first impressions.

An old rule of carpentry is to measure twice and cut once. The cut will be permanent, so make sure the cut is where you want it. Likewise, a first impression will be permanent—or changed only by an enormous expenditure of time and energy—so make sure that the first impression you make on someone is the one you want.

That gap between the dream and reality is what makes people miserable.

Everyone dreams of entering a room like a winner. Unfortunately for most people, that dream doesn't match reality. In real life, many are unsure of their direction, and wondering what they should do with their lives. They look for guidance haphazardly, looking in the wrong places and receiving the wrong answers. They often don't even realize the extent of their lack of direction.

That gap between the dream and reality is what makes people miserable. They want to be—or know they should be—in a better situation in life but can't figure out how to get there, or even where "there" is. When reality and expectations—or dreams—differ, misery is often the result.

Wouldn't it be great if everyone could shine through that first impression? If they possessed a sense of purpose and direction that emanated from them? If their happiness was so deep and pure that they couldn't contain it? That's the true power of a great first impression.

Let's talk for a moment about happiness. It's the defining emotion that everyone works so hard to achieve, so it's important that we have at least some idea of what we're talking about.

First of all, happiness is not winning the lottery or some other wish fulfillment via a magic lamp or a genie. There's an ancient curse that says, "May you receive everything that you wish for." The ancients (whoever they were) knew something about human nature. They understood that our nature is to strive and overcome. Earliest man had to hunt his food so he could eat. Later he learned how to grow crops, so he had to plant seeds and nurture plants so that he could eat. He had to work for everything.

It became part of our genetic makeup to associate effort and purpose with happiness. It was only after people began to have leisure time that they could afford the luxury of indulging in thoughts of magic lanterns and wish-granting genies and leprechauns. Unfortunately, in our modern society, we have become used to luxuries and an easy lifestyle. The daydream of "effortless happiness" has spread until it is the main preoccupation of many people.

While it may be momentarily pleasant to indulge in such fantasies, true happiness can't come from good fortune that drops in your lap. The inevitable question becomes, "Then what?" Although good fortune does happen, it should be treated as a tool to help you achieve true happiness and not the source of happiness itself.

Along with this idea is the notion that in order to have true happiness, you must have expectations. When our ancestors chased small animals for food, they expected to catch them. When our ancestors planted crops, they expected the plants to grow. Simply put, we have the capacity to understand that if we do this then that will happen.

Note the requirements of an expectation: it's an action/reaction, stimulus/response, cause/effect transaction. If it doesn't have these components, then it's simply a wish. An expectation is the result of something. Expectations require action.

One of the worst things that can happen to a person is to have no expectations. Many people are unhappy because they see no connection between their own actions and desired results. That disconnection is a result of years of conditioning by society. As strong and prevalent as having no (or low) expectations is, this goes against our natural inclination to strive and produce.

True happiness is not simple contentment. Animals feel content after they eat. You can feel content watching a sunrise or sunset. Enjoying the embrace of a loved one can lead to contentment.

A good meal, a beautiful nature scene, a sign of affection—these are all wonderful, and we should enjoy such things. What they are not, in and of themselves, is true happiness. They are the fruit and by-products of true happiness. You'll always want to stop and enjoy such moments, but don't confuse contentment with happiness.

As you can probably tell, I define happiness as something to be achieved. If we understand that happiness is when our expectations meet reality, then we have the ability to change either our expectations or our reality. That ability to change makes all the difference.

One of the factors that makes happiness possible is forward movement—the sense that we're actually progressing toward a goal. It's in our language—if a plan is progressing, we say it's "getting somewhere." If we want to execute a plan, we're "moving forward." A person who is successful is "going places." Simply sitting still is stagnation, and stagnation leads to disillusion and disappointment.

So movement is a requirement for happiness, and the degree of that happiness is measured by the velocity of your movement. Although many factors may be outside your control, your velocity is something you can control. By focusing your energies and knowing your purpose, you have the ability to achieve your happiness at a speed that you may have only dreamed about previously.

I remember learning an important concept in physics class at Montana State University. It says that when velocity is high, pressure is low. How true this is in so many situations in life. The situations and concerns that can derail us when we are just starting out become immaterial when we achieve velocity and momentum.

For example, let's consider two people, one earning $50,000 a year and the other earning $30,000 a year. Because of circumstances, the one earning $50,000 has to take a pay cut down to $40,000. He's miserable. Meanwhile, the one earning $30,000 gets a promotion and a raise and has a new salary of $40,000 a year. He's ecstatic. With the same income, two people have completely different outlooks because of their expectations and their movement.

You can tell from the example that achievement is part of being happy. It's the sense that you're moving in the direction that you want to go and that you're reaching goals that you've set for yourself. If you have no goals, you can never reach them. As Yogi Berra said, "You've got to be very careful if you don't know where you're going, because you might not get there."

By our nature, human beings want to achieve things. We've developed measurements of all kinds to help us measure our achievements. We have markers to show us how far we've walked, clocks to tell us how long we take on a task, and scales to indicate how much we weigh. If movement, which is necessary for happiness, means we're heading for a goal, then achievements are our ways of measuring how close we are to our goals.

Look at it this way—if a person never has any sense of achievement, then he can only wonder why he bothers getting up each morning. There's no reason to strive for excellence, no reason to stand out from the crowd, no reason to grow as a person. Each moment is a dull, gray interlude before he dies. There is no joy in life with all its attendant beauty.

Why do some people seem to grasp happiness, yet so many wallow in a pit of despair and disappointment? It has to do with programming. Programming is the messages you've received that have imprinted themselves on your subconscious, molding the type of person you are. In order to understand how this works, it's important to know how this programming is created.

Early Experiences

CHILDREN ARE NATURALLY TRUSTING, and they believe everything they're told. Because of the trust you felt as a child, the things you were led to believe at a young age still seem true to you. Without the protective armor of experience and caution that most of us develop as we get older, children take everything they're told to heart—especially anything regarding themselves.

Add to that the fact that you have held a belief for a large portion of your life, and you have an image or opinion of yourself that has taken root deep in your subconscious mind. It feels truer to you than information you might have received later in life. Consequently, those impressions, whether they're accurate or not, have a strong hold on you.

For example, what color is a yield sign? Many baby boomers might say yellow, but they were changed from yellow to red and white almost 40 years ago. We stop actually observing and spend too much of our time on autopilot.

Traumatic Experiences

MANY OF US ARE affected our entire lives by traumatic events that happened when we were children. If you're irrationally afraid of birds, dogs, balloons, clowns, or some other object that should be innocuous, then the cause may be a traumatic experience that happened to you when you were young.

If that fear is imposing on your life—you can't enjoy the circus with your children because you're afraid of clowns—then you've received programming that will keep you from reaching your potential.

Trauma is a moment of intense physical or emotional duress. During such a time, our minds are susceptible to suggestion. Especially when we are young and have not developed the mental defenses to protect ourselves, the effects of trauma can be amplified and permanent.

Social Experiences

WHEN WE ARE OLD enough to go to school, we spend more time interacting with our friends than we do with our own family (assuming you're not homeschooled). The sheer amount of time adds importance and weight to the impressions our friends have on our self-image.

Are there any of your old school friends who still go by the nicknames they were given in grade school? Do the nicknames still fit? Unless you were a television star, most childhood nicknames are not usually beneficial to an adult trying to achieve success.

Especially in grade school, children are brutally, often cruelly honest. Each of them is establishing his or her place in the pecking order and working to fit in with a particular clique. These efforts often come at the expense of another child. The pressure to conform to what others think we should be is tremendous. This sets in while we're in school and now controls us in the real world. Although all of us have had embarrassing moments in our lives, it's particularly damaging when that moment becomes an imprint that can last for years.

Silent Experiences

OF THE THOUSANDS OF communications we go through as human beings each day, the vast majority of them are nonverbal. The roll of the eyes, the crumpled mouth, the dismissive wave of a hand—these can affect you more than the harshest words.

Take, for example, this scenario: a woman is speaking to her husband and his arms are crossed. The common—but not entirely accurate—knowledge that many people have about body language would suggest that he is defensive, or close-minded, about what the wife is saying.

These may all be true, but he might just be cold. Or it might be a comfortable position. Now think of the anxiety it can cause in the relationship if the wife misinterprets the husband's posture as something it's not. Nonverbal cues are misinterpreted all the time, yet they affect us dramatically in the way we perceive ourselves and the people around us.

This is another reason why I teach basic body language reading skills. It is an entire language that we must understand to be more effective in any social or business encounter.

Who are the culprits that have damaged us with poor programming? I refer to them as the four P's—Parents, Professors, Preachers, and Politicians.

Parents

THE RELATIONSHIPS WE HAVE with our family members are the most important and influential relationships of our lives. Because of the strong emotional ties we have with family members, their opinions carry more weight than anyone else's, especially when we're young.

We depend on our parents to provide us with the necessities of life—food, clothing, and shelter. More important, though, is the emotional support that creates a healthy outlook on life in our later years. Mothers and fathers are usually untrained, and blunder through child rearing with the same faulty programming with which they themselves were raised.

Of course, they do the best they can. I have told my mom on more than one occasion that "she done good" with us kids. I hope to be as caring and understanding as my parents were when my time comes to be a parent.

This is why abusive relationships are so damaging. If a mother tells a child that he or she is "no good" or "stupid"—you get the idea—that child can carry the impression the rest of his or her life. The insult becomes a part of everything that person does from then on.

Professors

BY NOW YOU PROBABLY see the trend. People in positions of authority hold considerable influence. For impressionable young people, few have as much impact as their teachers and professors. We spend thousands of hours listening to them speak, and mixed in with the material we're required to learn is the subtle message, "This is what you should believe."

This influence may be as broad and obvious as a teacher mixing his political or religious beliefs in with the lesson. College students are especially susceptible because they are at the age when they are looking for their own way and questioning everything around them. For most of them, it's the first time they've been independent from their parents, so they naturally question what they may have learned at home.

On the other hand, the impact may be as personal as the professor making the student feel stupid or inferior. Many professors are known for their disregard for student's feelings, and make remarks about a student's work that can cripple a young person emotionally. A professor often looks at the end result of a student's work, not the amount of effort that went into producing it. When a student submits work that he has toiled over with all his abilities and skill, a professor's unkind remarks can cause tremendous emotional damage.

The professor holds a position not only of authority, but of learned authority. If the professor is teaching college, then he must be smarter than everyone else—or so the reasoning goes. When we hold this kind of template for the professor, then whatever he says will have a greater impact on us than it realistically should. We assign unreal levels of wisdom and judgment to the professor's opinion.

Preachers

ALTHOUGH MINISTERS, PRIESTS, AND other religious leaders receive training in their particular fields, they are still only human, with all of the frailties and shortcomings that being human carries with it. Sometimes they themselves get lost because of their own programming. Their own prejudices, biases, and likes or dislikes taint the spiritual message that they carry.

We rarely realize that our spiritual leaders are human, thus we take everything they say to heart. So while we're looking for spiritual guidance from these influential leaders, we are open to the faulty programming that they may slip into the message, either intentionally or accidentally. We allow them to have a moral authority that may not be fully deserved.

This is not a blanket condemnation of all spiritual leaders, of course. But too many of them add unnecessary guilt or prejudice to our burdens rather than the uplifting feeling of spiritual enlightenment. This message has a major effect on our own programming.

Politicians

IN AMERICA, WE ELECT most of our leaders. We presumably elect those individuals who have the best judgment as well as our best interests in mind. Unfortunately, our elected leaders have feet of clay, just like the rest of us. Because of their position, however, they hold a tremendous amount of power over the rest of us.

Laws and regulations rule our lives. Some control adds to an orderly society. When there are impositions into our personal freedoms, these laws cross the line. Intrusive legislation changes everything we do and limits the choices that we have at our disposal. These rules don't always pertain only to law and order.

The old saying goes that "You can't legislate morality," yet politicians often try to do exactly that. Using the microphone that accompanies being an officeholder, they often attack as immoral any behavior that doesn't conform to their own standards. Whether the charge is correct or not, the message seeps into our psyche and affects our own programming. Decisions that we would have previously made based only on the facts are now clouded by the politicians' mandates of what's right or wrong. We have allowed them to affect our programming.

In addition to parents, preachers, professors, and politicians, poor or incorrect programming causes destructive feelings that hinder us from achieving the potential that each of us holds within us. Loosely defined as a "feeling of apprehension or fear," anxiety has been programmed into many of us, causing us to worry about things we have no control over and, in many cases, that don't affect us anyway.

According to the Anxiety Disorders Association of America website, anxiety disorders are the most common mental illness in America. More than forty million adults suffer from some form of anxiety. For many people, worry takes control of their lives and restricts their options and the happiness available to them.

Often the anxiety bursts out into a full-fledged panic attack, where the person may feel like they're dying—pounding heart, difficulty breathing, even feelings of light-headedness. When this happens, the person's world stands still, and their entire life suffers. Work or relationships become secondary to containing this feeling of impending doom.

When a physically healthy person suffers from such an attack, we can see the profound effect that the mind has on the body. When a person has reached such a point, they have allowed someone else to dictate not only their mental health, but also their physical health.

Depression manifests itself in many ways, from simply having "the blues" to full-fledged suicidal thoughts. Although depression is often caused by an imbalance in body chemistry, the mind affects the body as much, or more than, the body affects the mind.

Many people have allowed joy to be removed from their lives by other people. It may be from the constant emotional grinding down from a family member or coworker. It may be from an unreal idea and feeling of failure to fulfill a parent's dream. It may be because we set expectations that are unrealistic in our jobs, relationships, or finances.

The number of ways that disappointment and low self-esteem destroy our lives are too many to count. The causes are everywhere, and without good programming, a person may not have the tools and the strength to fight off the feelings of depression. The drug industry sells numerous products to help fight depression, but it takes work to root out the programming that causes it in the first place.

A general malaise can take over our lives if we let it. Without a physically, emotionally, and mentally healthy outlook, we can suffer from a sense of failure, discontentment, or lethargy. If you've ever heard someone say "why bother?" then you will recognize malaise.

Programming often convinces us that we have no control over our lives. The thinking—if you can call it that—is that our lives are controlled by some mysterious force and that we have no control over our own destinies. When a challenge presents itself, instead of working hard to accomplish what needs to be done, the person will say "why bother?" and give it a half-hearted try. Then, when failure occurs from lack of effort, he points to it as proof of his theory.

It's no wonder that so many people feel like failures in their lives. Whereas they may have had high aspirations as children, they have been pulled down by the poor thinking going on all around them. Without a strong desire to achieve something, they simply give up and blame it on forces beyond their control.

The saddest thing in the world is those people who are dying young, yet still walking around breathing. They've given up on their hopes and dreams and are resigned to spend the rest of their lives waiting for the moment when they have to crawl into their graves and have dirt shoveled onto them.

Why do we give so much power to others? Why do we turn our emotional well-being and physical health over to people who are ill-equipped to advise us and who don't have our best interests at heart? The short answer is, we don't know any better.

Just as the weather affects all of us, we're affected by the wave of interactions we have with other people. Unless you live on top of a mountain and grow your own food, you're going to interact with others. Each of those interactions affects you, and if you've never learned the tools to create the life you want, then you merely react and give other people the power.

Although we don't fully understand why, our brains have a perfect memory. Sure, you may not remember what you had for breakfast this morning, but your brain retains that information whether you can access it right this minute or not. People with head injuries have been able to remember in minute detail events that happened years before.

That perfect memory retains information from a time before you can consciously remember. Physical and emotional traumas are stored in the back of your mind, affecting everything you do. You don't have a choice in this particular matter—your subconscious and your body remember for you.

You also have an enormous set of embedded beliefs. These beliefs can be about you personally (I have a bad temper because I'm Irish), or they can be about other people (people from the South are slow-witted). You might have a set of beliefs that even affect what you eat (never eat fish with dairy products).

Every culture and society is defined by its set of beliefs and social practices based on those beliefs. Although usually harmless, they nonetheless affect each of us in our daily lives. We unconsciously make decisions based on those beliefs. The harm comes when the set of embedded beliefs prevents us from making decisions or taking actions that move us closer to our goals.

If you refuse to work with certain people—the Irish, or people from the South, for example—based on these beliefs, then you are limiting the number of options available to you. Restricting your options without good reason is a sure way to limit your success. Although you cannot control the belief system of an entire culture, you can work to reduce the negative effects that those beliefs have on you.

We also observe and judge events based on a filtered outlook. We refer to this as our perception. This is the glass half-full or glass half-empty phenomenon. We perceive reality in a certain way because of the outlook we have been trained to have. Although events are neutral, the effect that they have on us is often based on our outlook, so we perceive them to be either negative or positive.

The options are not restricted to being an optimist or a pessimist. More and more we belong to the "television tribe," where television programming influences our outlook. Advertising is based on this one concept, the idea that our lives lack something and that only the advertised product can make us as happy, as cool, as healthy, or as beautiful as the people in the commercials. We are programmed to think that everyone else has the newest car, the newest gadget, or the newest, shiny object, and that our lives are lagging behind.

Television shows affect us the same way. Because characters in a series are in our homes regularly, we begin to think that we know them. The lives that they lead become the norm. We create expectations in our world based on the fictitious lives of people on television. Is it any wonder that so many of us are unhappy when we think the justice system works like *Law and Order* or that people in New York live like the characters in Friends?

We use poor perception mixed with poor information to decide the most important aspects of our lives.

Have you ever watched the Westminster Kennel Dog Show on television or even better, attended in person? Different breeds of dogs are paraded around for the judges. Based on years of experience and training, the judges note the physical and temperamental characteristics of the dogs and choose a winner.

If we made our decisions in such an informed way, we would rarely make mistakes. Unfortunately, most of us make decisions based on imperfect judgment. We use poor perception mixed with poor information to decide the most important aspects of our lives. Where we work, what we want out of life, and who we choose to spend our lives with are left to chance and to impulse.

Such haphazard decision making is what leaves us open to even more programming. If we don't have the discernment to know if an action is rational or not, then anything that sounds good at the time appears reasonable. Human beings, by nature, are lazy in their thinking, and it's easy to rely on programming rather than go to the effort of making the decision.

When you put all of these things together, what you find is an entire class of people with few alternatives. Through a combination of poor programming and poor choices, they feel as if they have messed up their lives and can't find a way out.

The statistics are clear. According to a recent *Time* magazine article, two-thirds of Americans are overweight, and half of those have graduated to full-blown obesity. One in six children ages six to nineteen are overweight, and even our pets are fat. Obesity is an equal opportunity condition, encompassing all races, economic classes, and both genders.

Obesity increases the risk of heart disease, high blood pressure, stroke, diabetes, infertility, gallbladder disease, osteoarthritis, and many forms of cancer. According to the Surgeon General website, the total annual cost for obesity in 2000 was $117 billion a year and climbing.

Our mental health isn't any better. According to the National Institute of Mental Health, an estimated 26.2 percent of Americans eighteen or older suffer from some form of mental disorder.

This physical, mental, and emotional deterioration comes at a huge cost. The Centers for Disease Control says that in 2005, visits to doctors' offices resulted in 2 billion drugs ordered or provided. Seventy-one percent of visits involved drug therapy, with the most common drugs being antidepressants. The Kaiser Family Foundation estimates that in 2005, Americans spent $200.7 billion on prescription drugs—almost five times the amount spent in 1990.

News and magazine articles constantly quote surveys showing how unhappy Americans are with their lives, including issues with government, the economy, their jobs, and their finances.

We drink too much, smoke too much, gamble too much, and take too many drugs, all in an attempt to anesthetize ourselves, so we don't have to face the pain of our lives.

The shame of it is that we didn't start out that way. When we were children, we laughed and played, looking at the world with unwavering hope and optimism. We dreamed of being and doing great things. Think about all the boys who had a poster of a Lamborghini on their bedroom walls. The world, as they say, was our oyster.

Then real life happened. In order to make your way in the world, you had to hide your individuality and conform to other people's wishes. You had your heart broken a few times and realized that relationships were much more work than you had anticipated. The job that you took to pay the bills—even though your training, education, and degree were in a completely different field—eats away at your self-esteem and your time.

Payments on your home, car, insurance, and all the stuff in your life, start to drag you down. Instead of enjoying your possessions, all you can think about is your bills. The destructive, financial duo of debt and abused credit combine to ruin even your paydays because there's never enough money.

The merchants and advertisers and the credit industry have worked hard to put a siphon into your bank account. It's sad to say, but it looks as though they are winning, and the public is losing.

As you've gotten older, you may have come to believe that success just happens to those who are lucky, and you will never have good enough luck to make it big. Slowly, you have started to give up. You rationalize that "that's just the way life is." Little by little, you have decided to let life pass you by while you just go through the motions.

Does any of this sound familiar? If it does, don't feel like you're alone. The bulk of people in the world today are just like you. It's not even a new phenomenon—Henry David Thoreau said in 1854 that "the mass of men lead lives of quiet desperation."

The truth is, it doesn't matter how common the problem is. That fact won't help you improve your life. What you need is an understanding of how you're going to get out of the downward spiral that you might be in now. You need something to help you bridge that gap between your reality and the dreams you should be dreaming.

Profile: Tiger Woods

TIGER WOODS IS FAMOUS for the number of championships he has won. He seemed destined for golf stardom at a young age. He even watched his father Earl hit balls into a net from his crib! Tiger appeared on television at age two, putting with Bob Hope. At age three, he shot a 48 for nine holes and appeared in golf magazines at age five.

Tiger went on to win many junior and amateur championships, setting records for being the youngest, winning the most, and having the best scores in golf tournaments. After he played in his first professional tournament in 1992, Tiger continued to improve, and in 1997, at the age of twenty-two, he won four PGA Tour events and was the leading money winner.

Tiger's dominance has been so complete that he is automatically the favorite when going into a golf tournament. Besides his natural skills and lifelong training, he has a focus that is almost beyond comprehension for the average person.

This focus was highlighted during the 2008 U.S. Open. Against medical advice, Tiger entered the tournament less than two months after having knee surgery, and he was clearly in pain as he limped through the course. On the final day of regulation play, Tiger tied Rocco Mediate to force an eighteen-hole playoff.

The two battled back and forth for the entire day, and Tiger grimaced in pain with each shot. Tiger was behind until the eighteenth hole, when he once again pulled even and tied the playoff. This led to a sudden-death playoff, which Tiger won on the first hole. After playing ninety-one holes of golf, he had won his third U.S. Open Championship.

After his win, it was revealed that Tiger had suffered a double stress fracture in his leg two weeks before the tournament. He also had surgery afterward to repair a torn ACL. To quote one news story by ESPN, "Woods managed to win a major that required five days of flinching, grimacing, and a long list of spectacular shots that have defined his career."

Tiger Woods shows what a true champion can be when facing adversity when skills, natural gifts, and hard work are not enough—the focus and heart to play through the pain and win.

Points to Remember

People can tell when you have confidence and know how to win.

The first impression you make on people determines how they interact with you.

Most people's dreams don't match their reality.

The gap between dreams and reality is what makes most people miserable.

Happiness is something you achieve.

True happiness requires movement.

Certain experiences—childhood, traumatic, social, and silent—make us vulnerable to programming.

Poor programming from the four Ps—parents, professors, preachers, and politicians—is the reason most people are unhappy.

Many mental, emotional, and physical ailments can be caused by poor programming.

We're susceptible to programming because our subconscious mind has a perfect memory.

We observe and judge events inaccurately because of our embedded beliefs, filtered outlook, and imperfect judgment.

We need something to help us bridge the gap between reality and the dreams we should be dreaming.

Chapter Two

Mind Power

–MIND POWER–

"We cannot always control our thoughts, but we can control our words, and repetition impresses the subconscious, and we are then masters of the situation."

— Florence Scovel Shinn

Why does my mind always seem to work against me?

How do I control my thoughts?

Are there different kinds of thoughts?

What forms our beliefs?

What is a paradigm, and how does it affect us?

A penny for your thoughts? How many times have we heard this or even said it? Considering that you can't buy anything for a penny these days, it doesn't place a lot of value on one's thoughts. This is a shame and a mistake because the thoughts you have determine what kind of person you are and what kind of life you lead. In fact, it's not an overstatement to say that the human mind is the most powerful force on the planet.

Consider this—every great human accomplishment, from the invention of the wheel to placing a man on the moon to the development of powerful computers that fit in the palm of your hand, have originated with a thought. The idea of creating something new, something that doesn't already exist, is an astonishing feat. It's the ability to see a gap in life and imagine a bridge of some kind to fill that gap.

This ability is unique to human beings. Beavers build dams and birds build nests, but these actions are based on instinct, genetically passed from generation to generation. They are not the products of conscious thought or creation. In contrast, it's hard to argue that the idea for the Apple iPhone was bred into all of us. It was the brainchild of one person, which then grew into what we hold in our hand today. Only humans can take different concepts, blend them together in a new way, and conceive something entirely different from what has existed.

Can you see why the person who pays you a penny for your thoughts could be getting quite a bargain? Your thought could potentially be worth millions of dollars.

Of course, some thoughts are more valuable than others. The value of a thought is the impact it has on improving your life. While all of us are capable of thought, the quality of those thoughts varies considerably from person to person. It's important that we understand the different types of ideas and their relative value.

Fleeting Thoughts

AT THE BOTTOM OF the thinking scale are random thoughts that flash through your mind. All of us have these—daydreams, disconnected images, or stray lyrics from a song are all examples of fleeting thoughts. This type of thought is characterized by its randomness and lack of connection from one thought to another.

Although these thoughts are common to everyone, they are usually just a result of sensory input. In other words, we hear a few notes of music, and it reminds us of a song we know. A cloud may look like an animal, or we may stare lazily at a running stream of water, without any real direction to our thoughts.

Fleeting thoughts offer little in the way of value to our lives. If a person spends too much time in this stage of thought, he will often wonder where the time went. Taken to an extreme, he might ask where his life went. The answer: it was spent wasted in nonproductive thought.

One of the dangers of video games to our children is that they encourage this type of thinking. Although at first, a video game might stimulate interest in strategy or learning rules, after a child becomes proficient, the controllers are manipulated by instinct with little conscious thought involved. Watch the faces of children as they play video games, and you'll often see that they have a blank expression. They are not thinking; they are simply responding to stimuli provided by the game.

Reflective Thought

ON A MUCH HIGHER level is the type of thinking that involves connected ideas. Reflective thoughts are based on a grasp of cause and effect, sequence, contrast and comparison, or commonality among different factors. Based on more than just sensory input, these thoughts relate to other thoughts, which lead to other thoughts and so on.

It's important to note that reflective thoughts are simply a more developed stage of fleeting thoughts. Daydreaming and fantasizing are the first steps in a process that leads to something greater than the current reality. Although staying in the first stage for too much of your time is not beneficial, it is still necessary for you to be able to have material to use at the higher levels of thought.

Reflective thinking involves the concept of sequence or consequence— if this happens, then that happens. One thing happens after another. Or two things happen at the same time but for a particular reason and with a definite result.

This type of thinking sounds very scientific and dry, but it's the basis for all modes of human thought beyond the most basic level. Imaginative works are part of this process as well—we use our judgment to determine if a sequence of sounds is musical or if they are just noise.

We make up stories using cause and effect. Even fairy tales are based on this idea. The evil queen gave Snow White the poison apple because she was jealous of Snow White's beauty. Goldilocks fell asleep in Baby Bear's bed because it was just right. The best works of art have resonance—they invoke other ideas in addition to the works themselves.

Reflective thoughts are important, but are not the highest stage of thinking.

Beliefs

THE WAY WE LOOK at the world, the things that we know (at least as much as we can know anything) are true are called beliefs. These beliefs may be based on evidence that we have seen with our own eyes, or they may be based on testimony or tradition that we accept without direct proof. As unintuitive as it may seem, the beliefs that we hold without direct proof can exert a greater influence on us than any firsthand knowledge we may have.

Beliefs based on firsthand knowledge are based on evidence. This evidence may be based on your own experience. You may believe that a Ford is better than a Chevrolet because you've owned both and the Ford performed better. Another person may have the exact opposite experience and will argue with you that the Chevrolet is vastly superior.

Both of you know that you're right based on your individual experiences. This process of reaching a conclusion—establishing a belief—about an entire class of items based on a sample of those items is called inductive reasoning. Sometimes these conclusions are correct, sometimes they're wrong, and sometimes they're nothing but an opinion.

Inductive reasoning is valuable to science because scientists often base a theory on observations of a small sample of a phenomenon. Using the scientific method, they then conduct experiments based on those observations to see if the theory is correct because most of us are not scientists, we don't use the scientific method to test our conclusions. Based on our own experience, our observations become beliefs.

If you find enough information to support your opinion, then you establish a belief.

Occasionally, though, we will be interested enough in a subject that we will research the topic. If you have ever read a consumer magazine, listened to a review of a movie, or looked on the Internet to find out what other people thought about something you wanted to buy, then you have conducted your own research. Sometimes the research is scientific, and sometimes it's simply to see what other people thought. Nonetheless, you gather information on the topic and base your opinion on your research.

If you find enough information to support your opinion, then you establish a belief. This method is obviously a more informed way of constructing a belief than simply relying on your own experience. A greater number of examples provide a truer picture of what a situation is.

If you watched Tiger Woods play golf when he was having a bad day, and that was the only time you watched him, you might conclude that he wasn't that good a golfer. On the other hand, if you watched him win fourteen major championships, you might more accurately decide that he was a very good golfer. You use the greater number of examples as evidence to support your belief.

In these cases, you have established a belief based on conscious thought. You reached your conclusion through a process where you compared the validity of your belief against the evidence that you had on hand. A particular belief may be incorrect, but at least it's logical. It makes sense because it's based on reality, on direct proof.

In contrast, beliefs that are not based on direct proof are by definition illogical. It doesn't mean they're incorrect, it only means that they were based on something other than reason. You might expect that beliefs based on reason or logic, backed by research and experience, would be the stronger influence in our lives. But the fact that we hold these beliefs without evidence makes them even stronger.

One of the factors that affects unproven beliefs is imitation. Consider this parenting philosophy: If a child has been raised in a home where the parents believed in the motto "spare the rod and spoil the child," then spankings were likely a common form of punishment. When the child grows up and has children of his own, he will probably adopt the same philosophy.

Of course, the parent may have done research of some kind and come to the conclusion that spanking was the best form of punishment. That would be an exception. Almost everyone parents their own children the same way they themselves were parented. They saw the example from the time they were born until they moved away from home—the formative years when we as people are most impressionable. We imitate the examples that made the biggest impression on us.

Another factor is tradition. Religious beliefs often fall under this category. If your parents were Catholic or Jewish (or whatever religion), you are more likely to be the same religion as your parents. What's more, you will likely raise your own children in the same religion as well.

Simpler decisions, such as who takes out the trash or who hosts the family Thanksgiving dinner, are often based on tradition. You may have run into instances at your job where out-of-date procedures are followed that don't make sense. It's easy to fall into the trap of doing certain things because "we've always done it that way." Sometimes those actions are still valid, other times not. Consider this story of a bride's first dinner:

A young bride cooked her first dinner for her new husband one evening, baking a ham for them to eat. Before she put the ham in the oven, she carefully cut off each end. When her husband asked her why she did that, she said that that was how her mother did it. The next day she thought about the conversation and became curious herself.

She called her mother and asked about it, and her mother said that was the way her mother baked a ham. The young bride called her grandmother and asked her. The grandmother replied, "When I was young, our roasting pan was too small for an entire ham, so I always cut off the ends so it would fit into the pan."

The bride believed that cutting the ends off the ham was the best method for baking a ham because the technique had been passed from generation to generation. We all hold traditions in high regard because we trust the judgment of those who have come before us. Although, as the story illustrates, sometimes traditions become outdated because they no longer apply.

Religious beliefs illustrate how dearly we hold traditions. Wars have been fought because of different religious beliefs. While some people may research options and base their religious decisions on that research, most people adopt the religion of their forefathers. Based on that tradition, they make momentous, life-affecting decisions.

All of this is not to imply that traditions are wrong. As Tevye says in *Fiddler on the Roof,* "it's how we keep our balance." People use traditions to create stability in their lives that would be hard to achieve if every decision had to be researched and made solely based on logic. We use tradition to guide us through the turmoil and problems that life throws at us.

What we have, then, is a combination of programming, imitation, and tradition that establishes early on how we view the world. That world view, or paradigm, is the framework with which we make our decisions, live our lives, and become the kind of people we are. Both good and bad, these forces create us and mold us. We move in the direction that we're guided.

What is a paradigm? It's the model we use when we look at our world. We compare everything in our experience to what we expect to see, and our reactions are determined by that comparison. In our world, animals don't appear out of empty top hats, so when a magician pulls a rabbit out of his hat we call it magic. Our set of experiences colors everything we see.

To a goldfish, the bowl is the paradigm. Like goldfish, we live in bowls that are created by the programming, imitation, and tradition mentioned earlier. Just like the goldfish, there can be an entire world outside of our own paradigm. We are limited by our paradigms because of the prejudices and restrictions we've been programmed to observe.

The challenge is to first realize that a world outside of our own paradigm exists and then to see the opportunities available there. We want to change our paradigm to an expanse of the possibilities available to us. We want to break through the fish bowl and into the greater world outside.

Your paradigm affects you in ways you don't even realize. It affects the language you use. If you're working on an important project and something goes wrong, do you immediately declare, "I'm dead!" to the world around you? Or do you say, "No big deal. I'll take care of it?" Such a small everyday choice affects your ability to handle setbacks and the way people perceive you.

More importantly, in your own mind you have either exaggerated or minimized the effect the situation has on you. The language you choose to use—as part of your paradigm—affects your own mind more than that of other people. You can develop a self-identity as a can-do individual, or you can be the person who drops the ball at the slightest problem. Your paradigm determines what you choose to be.

You may be an individual who sees abundance all around you. The universe is full of abundant riches, enough for everyone. On the other hand, you may be an individual who sees the world as miserly, where if someone else wins then you lose. Whether you have a prosperity mentality or a poverty mentality is determined by your world view.

In the same way, your paradigm affects your vision. Not whether you can pass an eye test at the optometrist's office, but how you see the world around you. You may have seen the *Where's Waldo?* puzzles—some people have the knack for picking out the striped-sweater hero quickly, while others struggle.

You have blind spots of your own—everyone does. Have you ever had a friend tell you that someone you know is attracted to you? Your reaction may have been, "I had no idea!" That's the kind of blindness I'm talking about. There are all sorts of opportunities available to you, but your reaction, if you heard about them, would be, "I had no idea!"

Those limitations are the biggest flaws in the paradigms of most people. That world outside the fish bowl is visible to the goldfish, but they don't look that far. As far as they're concerned, the world ends at the edge of the bowl. We're fortunate, however, because as human beings we can grasp the concept that our fishbowl is made of clear glass, and if we can only think to look, we can see the possibilities on the other side of the glass. For most of us, the problem is not what you don't know—it's that you don't know that you don't know.

What kinds of paradigms are we talking about? In what parts of our lives are they affecting us? How about mentally? Do you think of yourself as intelligent? Is intelligence important to you? College professors naturally consider learning and education very important. The blue-collar worker without a degree may think it's a waste of time. Both of these outlooks are correct according to the paradigms of the people making the judgment.

You may have a paradigm in which physical well-being outweighs anything else. If you grew up in a household where the adults were obese and food was important, then you likely developed the paradigm in which being overweight was normal and, contrary to most medical evidence, in some cultures even considered healthy.

Have your parents or grandparents celebrated their fiftieth anniversary? If they have, then you may have developed the paradigm of commitment to relationships. On the other hand, if you grew up in a single parent home, you may view relationships as temporary, even disposable.

How about money? Does it seem like there's never enough? Is money a constant source of worry and anxiety? Maybe your family was well-to-do, and money was never talked about because there was plenty of it. Or maybe your parents were not wealthy, but they were wise with their money, and it seemed that there was plenty of it.

The subject of paradigms, or world views, is intricate. Besides an overall paradigm, each part of your life reflects your paradigm, and they overlap and intertwine. Some paradigms work for you while others don't. You're aware of some, and others are still invisible to you.

How do you go about identifying your own paradigms? The same way you learn about anything else—you ask questions. Only in this case, you are the expert. But what kind of questions do you ask? Where do you even begin?

One simple way is to take inventory of your attitude toward certain areas of your life. Think about your health, relationships, career, and money. To stimulate questions, try fill-in-the-blank statements. For example, on the subject of health, you might ask, "A healthy person is?" Possible answers might be physically fit, disease-free, someone who exercises daily, a vegetarian, someone who has medical insurance—of course there are an infinite number of answers. Any of these suggestions might work, but the important thing is that the answer feels right to you.

Take some time with this exercise. You want to answer with complete honesty and with answers that feel right on a gut level. You might even devote a notebook or a file on your computer to your answers. Use your imagination to create statements that pertain to the different areas of your life. You might be surprised at some of the biases you've been carrying around without even knowing it.

Regarding paradigms, you should have two goals: to be aware of them and to adjust your paradigms so that you are living the best life possible. The exercise above can help you with the first part—but exactly how would you go about adjusting something as strong as your paradigm? The answer lies in your subconscious mind.

Oddly enough, with all that your conscious mind does for you, it's not the boss.

Earlier in the chapter, we explored how we have different levels of thought. Those are all part of your conscious mind. You have to use your conscious mind to get through your day. You have to read maps, decide what to have for breakfast, work on that report for work—the list goes on. Oddly enough, with all that your conscious mind does for you, it's not the boss.

The subconscious mind determines nearly everything you do, from running your body—you don't have to concentrate to make your heart beat—to creating hunches. The subconscious mind controls your world.

A recent study by a group of English and French neuroscientists, reported by Doug Bench in his book *Mind Your Brain,* determined that your subconscious mind determines the reward for every action. They monitored test subjects with brain imaging machines and flashed a series of images in front of them. They told the subjects they would be paid for squeezing a grip whenever they saw an image of money—larger amounts when the image was of a greater amount of money.

The images flashed for different lengths of time, some of them faster than their conscious mind could perceive. The scientists found that the test subjects squeezed the grip even when the image was too fast to see, and they squeezed the grip harder when the amount of money was greater.

The subconscious mind of the subjects was working to increase the reward without bothering to inform the conscious mind what it was doing. The scientists also saw that the subconscious mind used the same neural pathways as the conscious mind.

In other words, the subconscious mind makes decisions and occasionally tells the conscious mind what's going on. These decisions are in the ventral pallidum—sometimes called the reptilian part of the brain. Humans use this part of the brain because there are just too many decisions for the conscious mind to handle. Subconscious decisions are faster, and thinking about each and every decision on the conscious level can slow things down.

We obviously need both parts of our mind to function properly. Think of the subconscious mind as hot-wiring your brain—bypassing most of the machinery of decision making—and your conscious mind as the key to the ignition. Just because hot-wiring works, it doesn't make the key less useful.

More important than decision making, though, is the vast depository of—as Bob Proctor says—dormant resources available in your subconscious mind, waiting to be developed. If you can understand your subconscious mind, you can create giant gains in all aspects of your life, including improved health, loving relationships, material prosperity, and career satisfaction. To once again quote Bob Proctor, "Anything that you want to develop in your life or change in your life is just waiting for you to recognize that you can change it."

As a licensed Bob Proctor LifeSuccess coach, I couldn't agree more.

So our challenge is to put this powerful machine called the subconscious mind to work for us. Realizing that the subconscious and the conscious minds use the same neural pathways suggests that we can use conscious thought to influence our subconscious mind. We do this by changing our thought patterns.

It would be wonderful if implementing such a change was as simple as saying, "Thoughts, change yourselves." Unfortunately, human beings are a little more complex than that. Your subconscious mind developed its influence over the course of your entire life, so it works to resist change.

The thought patterns can be broken down into two categories: negative thoughts that work against us and move us away from our goals, and positive thoughts that move us toward our goals. We can work on these two categories to make the changes in our lives that we want. Obviously we want to reduce our negative thoughts and increase our positive thoughts. How is that done?

Negative thoughts hold us back. They can be something as blunt as telling yourself "I'm such an idiot!" when you make a mistake. They may be more subtle and manifest themselves as physical discomfort when something good happens to you. For example, how well do you receive compliments? Negative thoughts about yourself that you hold in your mind can make something as simple as receiving a compliment feel uncomfortable.

The first step is to recognize when a negative thought is occurring and interrupt it. According to Doug Bench, sports psychologist Dr. Jack Springer once worked with a quarterback who was underperforming because every time he made a mistake, he would criticize himself to the point that it interfered with his skills. Dr. Springer had the quarterback wear a rubber band on his wrist, and every time a critical thought intruded, the player snapped the band against his wrist. This physical interruption served to get the player's mind back in the place it needed to be so he could perform to his full abilities.

Often you can interrupt a negative thought by saying the word no. You basically refuse to give the thought permission to get into your head. Try it sometime when you find yourself dwelling on something in the past that went wrong. As soon as you recognize that you're thinking negatively, say no aloud. The stronger the thought, the more determined the "no" will have to be.

It's not enough to simply stop a negative thought. You also have to replace the thought with a positive one because the subconscious mind wants to have its way. For example, maybe you are trying to get physically fit, but you're stuck, thinking about the time that you missed a workout. Instead of dwelling on that thought, replace it with an image of you at the gym, maybe on the treadmill. Or imagine lifting a heavy weight, your muscles bulging with the effort. Those images show the person that you want to be, that you have to be, to reach your fitness goals.

Do this same exercise in all parts of your life when negative thinking drags you down. Use your imagination to demonstrate to your subconscious mind what a winner you really are.

Another step to decrease negative thinking is to avoid behavior that reinforces it. We all know someone who has a negative personality—unpleasant manners, a whiner, a complainer—you can compile a list of negative characteristics pretty quickly.

What you must actively choose is to not be that kind of person. Complaining about a situation or problem is nonproductive and merely gives vent to the negative thoughts. So does whining. What you want to do instead is turn the negative actions into positive ones. Instead of complaining about a situation, have a can-do attitude that silences your negative voice.

Another negative action that is more common, and even more destructive, is to obey the negative voice and become a quitter or, even worse, a person who doesn't start. That's the voice that whispers "you can't do this" or "it's too hard for you." Fight this voice with all your might. As Theodore Roosevelt said, "The man who really counts in the world is the doer, the man who gets things done, even if roughly and imperfectly."

Treat your negative voice like any other force that's trying to hold you back. Recognize it for what it is, and determine that it's not going to win. The negative voice is just the result of poor programming you have received. As we've seen, that programming can't always be trusted.

The next step is to increase your positive thoughts. Your positive thoughts generate an energy that affects everything else in your life. You may have had conversations with other people with attitudes—either yours or theirs. You'll probably remember the conversation as centering on performance. Having a good or bad attitude determines the way you function in your life.

We want to not only replace negative thoughts with positive ones, but also generate positive thoughts without having to deal with negative ones. By increasing the frequency and intensity of positive thoughts, we soon find that there's no place for negative thoughts any more.

Consider this story about a very well-respected karate master: A karate student with some experience and skill went to the martial arts master to ask if he could study with him. After having the student demonstrate what he could do, the master asked the student to join him at a table.

On the table were two glasses and a pitcher full of water. One of the glasses was nearly full of cola and the other full of water. The master pushed the glass with the cola in front of the student. "This is what you think you know about martial arts." Then he pointed toward the glass full of water. "This is what I know I know about martial arts."

The master poured water from his glass into the one with cola until the liquid was to the rim. "Because of what you think you know, there is very little room for what I know. The only way for you to learn is to release what you think you know and fill yourself with what I can teach you." The master poured more water into the glass until it overflowed. When his own glass was empty he took the pitcher and continued pouring.

Soon the glass that had been full of dark cola was almost clear. "As you can see, by replacing the thing that you already have with something that you desire even more, you can achieve whatever you want to achieve."

Think hard about the things you want, and find a positive image to replace the negative thoughts your subconscious mind can send you. You'll soon discover that negative thoughts will come less often.

Focus on your emotions and physical reactions when you consider images. Anything that you've been told you should do, but doesn't feel right to you, won't work. There's no fooling your subconscious mind. Only thoughts and images that generate genuine, pleasant feelings will be able to effectively replace your negative thoughts.

By controlling your thoughts, you control your life. As Marcus Aurelius said, "Our life is what our thoughts make it." Dwell on the positive, and positive things happen. By filling your mind with positive thoughts, you emit an energy that attracts good things to you. By consciously choosing what you will think, you begin a process in which you enter a new plane of existence.

Control your thoughts, and you control your feelings. Control your feelings, and you control your actions. By controlling your actions, you control your results and your life.

It's the power of thought that makes man the dominant creature on the planet. An ox is stronger, a lion has sharper teeth, and a cheetah is faster. Only our brains make it possible for us to fashion our world in such a way that we can survive and thrive.

When we use conscious effort to change our mindset through the force of positive thought, we take control of our destiny and dissolve the chains that others have bound us with through poor programming. We can overcome this programming, and any other obstacles, using the power of thought and the unlimited power of the mind.

Profile: Viktor Frankl

VIKTOR FRANKL WAS AN Austrian psychiatrist and brain surgeon in the early twentieth century. An acquaintance of Sigmund Freud and Alfred Adler, Frankl concentrated on the subjects of depression and suicide.

From 1933 to 1937, he headed the so-called Selbstmörderpavillon, or "suicide pavilion," of the General Hospital in Vienna, where he treated over thirty thousand women prone to suicide. Yet, starting in 1938, he was prohibited from treating Aryan patients because he was Jewish.

In 1942, Frankl, his wife, and his parents were rounded up with other Jews and sent to the Theresienstadt concentration camp. Frankl was separated from his family and herded into a barrack with hundreds of other men.

For three years, Frankl endured inhuman treatment by the Nazis. Men died around him from the punishment and the deprivation. Frankl saw that many of them simply gave up living and essentially willed themselves to die.

Frankl survived and helped others survive by seeing meaning in life. In his book *Man's Search for Meaning*, Frankl describes an occasion when his situation, punctuated by the numerous physical discomforts, nearly overwhelmed him:

"I became disgusted with the state of affairs which compelled me, daily and hourly, to think of only such trivial things. I forced my thoughts to turn to another subject. Suddenly I saw myself standing on the platform of a well-lit, warm and pleasant lecture room. In front of me sat an attentive audience on comfortable upholstered seats. I was giving a lecture on the psychology of the concentration camp! All that oppressed me at that moment became subjective, seen and described from the remote viewpoint of science. By this method I succeeded somehow in rising above the situation, above the suffering of the moment, and I observed them as if they were already of the past."

It was by using the power of directed imagination that Frankl was able to survive the horrors of the Nazi concentration camp. If you feel as though you are unable to reach heights far above your current grasp, think of Viktor Frankl and his ability to imagine himself far away from his physical existence, rising above the situation.

Although his family did not survive the concentration camps, Frankl himself went on to found the field of logotherapy and to become a leading figure in the field of existential analysis. The author of several books, Frankl continued writing and lecturing until his death in 1997.

Points to Remember

The human mind is the most powerful force on earth.

The value of a thought is the positive impact it has on your life.

There are different kinds of thoughts—fleeting thoughts, reflective thoughts, and beliefs.

What we "know" to be true often isn't.

The beliefs we hold are often based on programming, imitation, or tradition. These establish our world view, or paradigm.

Whether you have a poverty or a prosperity mentality is based on your paradigm.

Your paradigm affects all aspects of your life. It affects your relationships, health, career, and money.

The best way to discover the limits of your paradigm is to ask questions.

You should have two goals regarding paradigms: be aware of them, and adjust them so that you are living the best life possible.

For most of us, the problem is not what you don't know; it's that you don't know that you don't know.

*The subconscious mind is full of abundant
resources waiting to be developed.*

*The challenge is to use our intellectual faculties to
put the subconscious mind to work for us.*

*Replace negative thoughts with positive ones until
there's no room for negative thoughts.*

*Control your thoughts, and you control your feelings. Control
your feelings, and you control your actions. By controlling your
actions, you control your results and your life.*

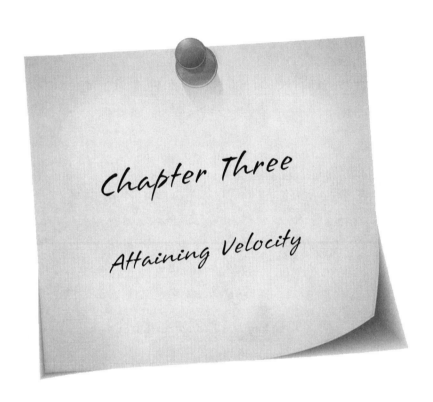

Chapter Three

Attaining Velocity

— ATTAINING VELOCITY —

"Nothing contributes so much to tranquilizing the mind as a steady purpose – a point on which the soul may fix its intellectual eye."

— Mary Wollstonecraft Shelley

How do I discover my purpose?

Why is having a purpose so important?

How do I decide what's important to me?

What are role models, and why are they important?

How do I use the power of focus?

The nineteenth century psychologist and philosopher William James once wrote, "The great use of life is to spend it on something that will make a difference." As we go through life, we all want to make a difference to our families, our friends, and the world. We all want to be remembered after we're gone.

So far, we've discussed how poor programming can hold us back and that we can counteract that programming by using conscious thought to influence our subconscious mind. At this point, you may feel that you're ready to set goals and get busy reaching them. However, there's a more important step first. You must ask yourself, "What's my purpose?" Your goals are what you want to achieve; your purpose is why you want to achieve those goals.

Your purpose is that force in your life that meets James's standard of making a difference. In his book *The 7 Habits of Highly Effective People*, Stephen Covey talks about someone who climbs the ladder of success only to find that the ladder is leaning against the wrong wall. Before you begin your journey of improvement, you need to make sure your purpose is clearly defined.

Why is establishing your purpose so important? First of all, it clarifies what you really want out of life. Human beings are susceptible to thinking that what is in front of them is the most important thing. Because of the job you fell into, because of the people you associate with, or because of activities or organizations that you accidentally became involved with, your picture of what's important can be skewed.

Like a warped mirror, your view has just enough truth in it to fool you. What you have been led to believe is right may indeed be right—but not for you. Through introspection and self examination, you can separate what you've been taught by other people from what you truly believe, but it requires that you actually do the work.

Clarifying your purpose is essential to moving in the direction you want your life to go. This is such a highly personal process that even your family or closest friends may not be the ones to help you. They have their own interests and purposes, which may not match yours. By establishing a clear purpose, your path to success will be much simpler to follow.

Having a clear purpose will also help you when things get tough. Any objective you set for yourself will inevitably involve some resistance from other people or simply from the world. If you are attempting something that is unique—even if it's only unique to people around you—the resistance will become greater the more you veer away from other people's expectations.

The resistance and pressure are greatest when you are just beginning something new. Many individuals have pursued their unique vision alone and against the advice of their family, their friends, and even the experts. Those who succeeded maintained their sense of purpose throughout their search for something new.

The irony is that very often the unique vision becomes accepted wisdom after it is successful. Those who opposed the idea can suddenly become ardent supporters, and jump on the bandwagon—after it's already rolling.

"Keep your eye on the prize," goes the old folk song. That song has helped people work through harsh treatment and bitter disappointments because they knew they were working for something bigger than the moment. Temporary obstacles will nearly always present themselves if you're working toward a worthwhile goal.

If you are simply living moment by moment, a small problem can be blown out of proportion by a negative mindset. But if you know that some challenges are inevitable as you follow your purpose, the issue can be considered for what it is—a necessary part of the journey.

To find your own special purpose, you will need to decide what's really important to you. Working for a large, important goal because of a worthy purpose gives you added momentum to achieve that goal. Deciding what's really important is based on your values.

One problem is that most of us have only a vague notion of what is important to us. Sure, it's nice to have money, someone to love us, and maybe good health, but beyond those few concepts, have you given any thought to your values or to the multitude of possibilities and their relative importance?

Let's take the three mentioned above—money, love, and health. Which of these is most important to you? Money? Would you be happy if you were a millionaire, and you only had a week to live? Probably not. So maybe good health is relatively more important than money?

The good thing about values is that they're not mutually exclusive. You can value wealth, love, and health. What's important is to realize that sometimes your values will bump up against each other, and you will be forced to decide which is more important.

Often your values will work together. "Hmmm, I value going to the beach, but I also value time with my kids. Ah, I know, I'll take the kids to the beach!"

The example above is a little silly because most of us make those judgments all the time without going through a step-by-step process. It's a great illustration, though, that the process does take place, even if it's subconsciously.

The danger when compiling your values list is that you may feel certain values should be important to you. Avoid this trap. No one else has lived your life. Siblings may share many of the same values yet differ in key areas. Even twins, who share so much in their lives, may have very similar values yet place different emphasis on those values.

Try to think of occasions where your emotions were highly charged, and see if it was because one of your core values was being violated, or conversely, if a core value was being observed. If instances come quickly and easily to you, then you're close to seeing the higher-priority values in your own life. Identifying your values helps you discover what your real purpose is.

Remember that establishing your purpose is the first step in the process. It gives you the why you need before you settle the what. For example, pretend you are salesman of medical supplies. If someone asked you why you do what you do, what would be your answer? "For the money" is the first thought that comes to mind, and it may be accurate. But let's continue with questions—if you could make the same amount of money doing something else, would you rather be doing some other kind of work?

Through a series of questions (and honest answers) to find out why you do what you do, you may discover that the deepest pleasure you get from your work is to help people. Helping people is a core value, one that can help you find your true purpose. Again, happiness is achieved by aligning your actions with your values, which in turn fulfills your purpose.

To clarify your purpose, create a one-sentence purpose statement for your life. This applies to several aspects of your life, but normally it involves your occupation—the thing that you do for which the world pays you. For example, a purpose statement might read like this: "My purpose is to attract and lead as many people as possible towards optimal health with natural chiropractic care." Or "My purpose is to help as many people as possible toward a healthy smile as a dental hygienist." Or "My purpose is to help as many people as possible enjoy the outdoors as a fishing guide in Glacier National Park." You get the idea.

My purpose is to_____

_____

_____

_____

_____

AFTER YOU'VE DECIDED WHAT your purpose is, it's time to unleash the power of your subconscious mind. One of the best ways to communicate with your subconscious mind is through the use of images and visualization. If you think about your dreams—one of the times when the subconscious mind is being more obvious about its communication—you'll realize that most dreams revolve around images. Pictures are the subconscious mind's native language.

To start the visualization process, go back to what we originally discussed—the gap between reality and your dreams. At this point, you're ready to bridge that gap. First, based on the work you've done on your values and your purpose, create your dream image. If creating wealth is your purpose, imagine what your life and your world would be like as you create enormous amounts of wealth for yourself and others. If being physically fit is part of your purpose, think about being strong and agile, your body able to accomplish any task you ask it to do.

Be as specific as possible with your images. Put as much detail as you can into what you see. Every accomplishment is achieved in the mind first. I'll never forget what Arnold Schwarzenegger said the first time I met him several years ago: "The body always follows the mind."

The body always follows the mind.

Creating a detailed scene in your mind gives the subconscious mind its orders—this is what I want. The subconscious mind accepts the imagery as true, and the clearer the picture, the deeper that acceptance goes.

Your critical conscious mind will try to interfere, but don't let it. You don't need to know how you'll achieve the image you create. All you need to do is create the reality in your mind that what you see will happen. Eliminate all doubt by imagining only the end result—you in the position you want. Napoleon Hill, legendary author of the long-time bestseller *Think and Grow Rich,* said over eighty years ago, "What the mind can conceive and believe, it can achieve."

If you interrupt your own dream with all the nagging, little questions of how, you'll soon find yourself sidetracked and dealing with small annoyances. Later in the process, you can deal with how to achieve your image, but for now, all you want is that clear picture of you doing, being, or having what you want the most.

So What Do You Want?

SOMETHING THAT MIGHT HELP you at this point is taking an inventory of your strengths. Compiling a list of all the things that are right about you reinforces your image of a stronger, richer, more successful you. Your self-image, self-esteem, and confidence will grow as you consider in detail your strongest assets.

If you've been beaten down so much by poor programming that you don't think you have any strengths, think about this: You're reading this book aren't you? Isn't that an indication that you have at least one positive trait— the desire to improve your life? If you have one positive trait, then odds are you have others.

What we're looking for is a systematic approach that will allow you to realize the resources that you already have available to you. Recognizing and using these resources will help you achieve your goals.

When companies want to know what resources they have—products, raw materials, widgets—they do an inventory. By knowing what they have on hand, they know what they need to acquire, and they know what goals they can achieve with what is already available. You can use the same technique to discover what you already have available to you. Once again, this process is essentially a series of questions.

Physical

ARE YOU HEALTHY? DORLAND'S Medical Dictionary defines health as "an optimum state of physical, mental, and social well being, not just the absence of disease or infirmity." Do you live a healthy lifestyle—eat right, exercise, etc.? Are you involved in sports or good at a particular athletic event? Maybe you're strong or very coordinated. Do you have good eyesight or a keen sense of smell? Can you hear a pin drop across the room?

Some of these questions might seem silly to you, but they're all part of your physical makeup. It's been said that we're not physical beings but spiritual beings on a physical journey. Your physical traits are the tools you have to work with on that journey.

Now's the time to be honest, not modest. Maybe you've got a great head of hair. Do you look good in your clothes? One man who performed this exercise wrote that he looks good when he wears a hat—that's the kind of detail you want.

As your list of physical attributes grows, occasionally stop to think about the physical limitations that some people overcome. Your potential is incredibly enhanced if you enjoy something as simple as good health. Realizing what wonderful physical benefits you have is a major part of creating that winning image.

Mental

HOWARD GARDNER, A PROFESSOR of education at Harvard University, in his classic work *Frames of Mind: The Theory of Multiple Intelligences,* defines intelligence as the potential ability to process a certain sort of information. The different types of intelligence are, for the most part, independent of one another, and no type is more important than the other.

As with physical attributes, there are many aspects to intelligence. While most people believe that being intelligent relates to having a high IQ, that is only one portrayal of intelligence. You may be verbally accomplished, musically inclined, or great with numbers. Any of these can be an aspect of intelligence.

Relationships

INTERPERSONAL RELATIONSHIP SKILLS IS another of Gardner's areas of intelligence. I've separated it from the mental section because it involves another skill set that depends on other people: the quality of your relationships. A frank and honest look at your relationships can reveal strengths that you didn't know existed in your life.

Are you skilled at communicating with other people? Do people seem eager to confide in you or to take you into their confidence? Is it easy for you to empathize with others and to see their point of view? Are you charismatic or a natural leader? Being able to work well with others, to collaborate on projects, can also indicate a high level of relationship skills.

As you look through the list of strengths that you already possess, imagine they belong to another person. Would you like that person? If you knew someone else that had all those attributes, would you admire him or her or even envy that person? Guess what...that person is you.

Creating the image of a successful you is easier when you realize that you have potential that you've scarcely touched. By knowing the why, and recognizing the incredible qualities that you already possess, you can create an image in your mind that is as solid and real as anything that has happened to you in the past. That's the type of visualization you want.

Another technique that's useful is to ask yourself what kind of person is already living the type of life you want. Who do you know that has already achieved the scene you are creating in your mind? If you're fortunate enough to have someone close to you that fits the description, you're in luck—you've found a role model.

The importance of role models can't be overstated. It is immensely difficult to achieve certain goals if no one you know has ever done it.

Besides the example they provide, role models can show you exactly how they accomplished their goals. Financial expert Dave Ramsey says that he actively sought out millionaires when he was younger, invited them to lunch, and plied them with questions on how they earned their millions. His motto is, "Find people who did what you want to do, and do what they did."

Our world is filled with role models, but not the kind that we want. Most of us are surrounded by people who have given up, who indulge momentary whims at the expense of larger goals, or whose lives are spent in indulging appetites rather than enriching their souls.

The challenge in using role models to help you further your development is finding the right ones. Seeking out those whose paths are similar to the one you want to follow can be difficult, especially if your path differs from the paths chosen by those close to you.

There are different ways to find role models whose examples can help you reach your own goals.

Seek Out Those Close to You

ALTHOUGH I PAINTED RATHER a bleak picture above, I didn't mean that there are no positive role models around you. If you want to be a good parent, look at your own parents. Find particular aspects of their parenting that worked and duplicate them. Even if you're not perfect, with time and practice, you will likely be able to duplicate their results.

Look around your neighborhood. There are those who may be great at listening, and you can learn from them. A restaurant's employees may provide fantastic service—seek out the owner or manager, and see what they did to train those employees.

Is there someone in your town whose reputation for being honest and honorable is spotless? Find them and buy them lunch. Find out the actions they took and the sacrifices they made to achieve that kind of reputation. The point is to seek out people geographically close to you who have accomplished the things that you want to accomplish and who have demonstrated the same values that you have.

Role Models from Afar

FOR MOST OF US, there are many role models whose exploits and accomplishments are in tune with our own goals but who we are not able to have face-to-face communications with.

Regardless of their sometimes high status, occasionally our heroes are close enough to make contact. A few years ago I was able to meet a childhood hero, Arnold Schwarzenegger, at a professional seminar. It inspired me to take my personal fitness even more seriously, as well as pursue my business goals.

Is your hero appearing anywhere nearby, perhaps to give a speech or some other presentation? Take the opportunity to attend, and if a question-and-answer session is available, take advantage of it. Although they can't usually give lengthy answers to your questions, they will often give you an insight to their own success.

Sometimes it can be as simple as writing a letter. Many accomplished people are willing to answer a politely written letter in which you explain your own goals and ask for advice.

If your hero doesn't respond to a letter, then try to read any articles or books he or she has written. Contemporary authors are often able to describe their story in more detail in a book. Biographies are also a great way to learn the story of your contemporary role model. Autobiographies are especially useful because they are written in the person's own words.

Biographies are sometimes the only way to learn the secrets of success of people from the past. Their life stories can be both an inspiration and an instruction manual for anyone wishing to learn from them.

Sometimes you'll be fortunate enough to find a whole series of books by an author that explains his or her philosophy. Napoleon Hill's books have become legendary in providing the precise tools that he uses and advocates in achieving success.

The Power of Your Imagination

YOU WILL OFTEN FIND that you're not able to reach just the right role model for what you're trying to accomplish and the life you're trying to lead. What should you do when you've run out of other resources? Use your imagination.

The concept of using your imagination to achieve your goals may be foreign to you. You may, in fact have, been told not to spend so much time in your imagination.

The use of your imagination is a double-edged sword. If you spend too much time daydreaming aimlessly about what-if situations, then you are actually squandering time and improperly using one of your most powerful tools.

When used properly, the imagination provides you with the power to tap into energy and other resources you might not realize you already have.

What we're advocating here is the planned, structured use of directed imagination. The difference between directed imagination and simple daydreaming is that you're consciously deciding to use some of the same techniques you use when daydreaming to work toward a specific goal. You're daydreaming with a purpose.

In this case, you're looking for a role model who has accomplished certain things, or achieved particular goals, or otherwise embodies the traits that you desire to possess.

First you want to do proper research. If you've searched locally to find a role model, and you've read books and articles to find a person either living or dead who could serve as a role model, then you've already been exposed to some people who exhibit traits similar to the ones you want.

You will be constructing a fully-customized role model, taking a piece from one person, another piece from someone else, and so on until you've made a model close to what you wanted.

One way to idealize your role model is to think of the actions the person would take. Ask yourself, how would a person act who had the traits I'm looking for? For example, someone who worked hard to earn a fortune, starting from nothing, might value earning more than someone who won the lottery.

Imagine your person looking over the phone bill to make sure he or she was charged correctly. Or you might imagine that same person as tired, discouraged, and wondering if the effort was worth it, but then they go to the next sales call anyway.

Let's stop and play with that last image for a moment. What you could do is imagine the next sales call going well and the feeling of triumph your model would have because they persevered. By using your imagination, you can actually feel the thrill of winning by overcoming obstacles.

Essentially you're asking yourself questions and then answering them. Instead of a shallow, easy answer, though, you are using the power of your imagination to dig deeper, in coordination with your values, to find the best answer. While in many cases your first instinct is right, in this process you want to dig for more meaningful concepts than just your first flash of inspiration.

Another way you can approach the imagined role model is to make yourself the role model—not the you that you are now but the you that you would be if you had the particular traits you're looking for. The question you can ask yourself is, "How would I act if I were that type of person?" Follow the same process as I described earlier by imagining not only the actual actions but the emotions that would accompany the successful exhibition of a particular trait.

Make sure that when you do this your imagined role model is actively exerting influence on the situation in question. A passive scenario, where your role model is merely the recipient of good fortune, falls back into mere daydreaming.

As you do this exercise, you will become more adept at entering the special mindset necessary to creating a realistic and effective scenario. Push yourself to make your role models more insightful and creative, looking for ways to make your sessions of directed imagination more productive.

Once you've established a clear image of exactly what you'll look like in your winning scenario, it's time to focus your energies toward making that picture a reality. This is the point at which you begin to eliminate the gap between reality and your dreams.

What is focus? The dictionary defines focus as "a central point, as of attraction, attention or activity." In this case, you'll focus your energies— your attention and activity—on a single goal, with the help of a special tool. By focusing like this you will be able to achieve much more than you ever thought possible.

Normally in day-to-day activities, we are distracted by anything that comes along. Every little problem becomes a major obstacle to overcome. If it's raining, you might grumble about having to wear a raincoat or carry an umbrella. You have to take extra time to drive to work because of poor road conditions. You get to work and your hair is wet. You start your work day in a bad mood.

But when you're focused on creating the mental image you've created, you don't have time to waste on trivial matters. You still have to use an umbrella and allot extra drive time. Your hair is still wet when you get to work. But now these are trivial matters that don't take up an inordinate amount of your energy or attention. You are focused on bigger objectives. When you fill your mind with the more important ideas, there is less room for the unimportant ones.

Have you ever bought a new car and suddenly noticed more of the same car on the road? It seems like everyone else had the same idea that you did and bought the same car. The truth is that the other cars were there all the time. The difference is that now you're paying attention, so there seem to be more of them.

In the same way, focusing your attention on creating your new reality will clarify the image. Points that might have been fuzzy before will sharpen. Vague details will become more specific. By spending more time thinking about your goal, the world will seem to fill with information that is pertinent to your goal. It will feel like you're attracting resources to you.

You will also begin to spend time on activities that will move you closer to your goal. Trivial time-wasting will vanish from your life as you work to get a bigger return on your time investment. Creating your new reality will overcome the desire to kill time. You'll discover that each moment is precious, and your actions will align themselves with your goals.

By focusing your attention and activities on creating the image you have created, a natural law will come into play—the universal law of attraction. You are adhering to the principle of this law by creating a clear picture of what you want more than anything else. You have decided to exclude unnecessary distractions.

As the universal law of attraction begins to work for you, you will see events in your life start to coalesce around your goal. Resources will become available to you unexpectedly, and seemingly random occurrences will work to your advantage.

You are simply taking advantage of a natural law that provides for those who adhere to it.

Keep in mind that you are not creating something new. You are simply taking advantage of a natural law that provides for those who adhere to it. By defining your purpose, feeling the desire to bridge the gap between reality and your dreams, and clarifying the image of yourself as the way you want to be, you have followed the path that others have followed before you. The law of attraction has always been there, and now you are in a position to use it. Remember, you can have anything you want in life, as long as it doesn't violate God's laws or interfere with the rights of others.

The role of focus is important here. Without focus, your energies are spread over a wider area, reducing the results in each of those areas. Your area of concern—those things that are on your mind—is nearly always larger than the area of your world that is under your control. Worrying about things over which you have no control is a certain path to disillusionment and frustration.

Concentrating on those things you can control, especially the activities and resources that are part of constructing your new reality, is more rewarding in the results you get and the emotional stability you'll enjoy. Rather than attempting a number of different activities with poor results, you focus all your resources on those that are most important to you.

The improved results will be apparent. Your time with your family will become more valuable. Think about it—how do you feel when you're having a conversation with someone and their attention is fully on you and on the conversation? One of the best compliments you can pay someone is to be totally attentive when they say something. That's the kind of impact you'll have on people when you discard trivial concerns and focus on the more important items in your life.

Just as an artist can achieve more detail in his creations when he is focused, you'll be able to perceive and enjoy the details of your life. By paying greater attention to such detail, you'll be able to enhance every aspect of your life because you will have achieved focus.

Of course, the greatest benefit to your new focus will be the realization of the image you've created. Incidental benefits will present themselves, so enjoy them when they come. The main thrust of your focus, though, is to specifically make the picture you've created and fulfill the purpose that is truly yours.

When we talk about focusing our energies, what are we really talking about? Remember that your subconscious mind is the most powerful force on earth, and that you are using your conscious mind to influence the subconscious mind. So you are focusing your mental energies on making your goal a reality.

When you have a specific goal in mind—whether it's to run a specific business, earn a certain amount of money, improve your health, or build a relationship—you must concentrate on that goal almost to the point of obsession. Any spare moments you have should be spent planning for the new reality you'll enjoy and preparing to take advantage of opportunities that present themselves to you.

Michael Jordan is arguably the best player the NBA has ever seen. He holds several records and was a crowd favorite for an entire generation of basketball fans. His superior ability and seemingly superhuman feats show what a truly gifted athlete he was.

Jordan's coach, Phil Jackson, discussed another side of Jordan in a recent ESPN article. He says that when Jordan first entered the league, he was one-dimensional, meaning parts of his game were not up to professional standards. Jordan worked tirelessly on the aspects of his game that were not as strong, spending hours in the gym on his days off. When it was game time, he soared above the other players in large part due to his focused energy on becoming the best player in the game.

Even though he was a talented athlete, Michael Jordan would not be the household name he is today if he had not worked hard to take advantage of the position his talents had gotten him. He practiced almost to the point of obsession. He had an image of himself as the best player in basketball history and focused his thoughts on that goal. In the same way, you must harness your thoughts so that your goal is as important to you as Jordan's goal was to him.

Another lesson to be learned from Michael Jordan is the importance of shaping your world and your environment around your goal. He didn't sit at a table eating pie, simply wishing he could be a great athlete. He spent his time in the gym where he could actively exert effort to realize his dream.

You must likewise form an environment that is conducive to your goal. Why is this approach important? Because you want to give yourself every chance to succeed. You want to create a successful environment. You'll be engaged in a hard—sometimes very hard—quest for self-improvement, and during this time, you'll enjoy contentment and mental congruity if you realize that your goals are worthy and that you are worthy of the effort you'll be putting into the quest.

As you go through this process, there will be times when you will be more vulnerable to negative influences. A misinterpreted look or an inadvertent remark from a loved one can throw you off track. Take this opportunity to surround yourself with positive things that create a good feeling. Do you enjoy a particular flower? Put it in your office. Is there a painting or photograph that inspires you? Hang it on a wall where you can see it often. Do you have a certificate of achievement or some other sort of recognition that you're proud of? Put it in a prominent place.

At the same time, get rid of items that make you feel bad. Is there a portrait of a person or scene that depresses you? Either get rid of it entirely or put it someplace where you won't have to look at it. Do you have a pile of old magazines or books that you have put off reading, and now you feel guilty? Same thing.

In my coaching, one of the first things we do is unclutter your life. If you haven't worn it in the last year—get rid of it. If you have no immediate use for it, just give it away. We must make room for the new and better.

The idea is to actively design your world so that positive influences dominate. By creating this environment, you'll be able to see more clearly what great things you are capable of achieving.

Books, CDs, tapes, and videos can be great sources of inspiration and instruction. The wisdom and knowledge of the entire world can be at your fingertips. Biographies, histories, essays, commentaries—you never know when a passage will reach you and provide the spark that lights a fire inside you. You may have to sift through tons of information to find the one bit that speaks to you, but it's worth it when you find it.

Whether you have a private office or have to use the kitchen table, try to carve out a space that is your "success space." Clear everything else out of the way and devote that portion of your world to your quest to realize your new reality.

As with many of the other techniques, repetition of this particular routine is designed to create a habit—the success habit. When you sit in your chair at your special place, you should feel like you're a master craftsman designing your life and your future. That is, in fact, what you are—your own life expert. You know your situation and what you need better than anyone else. Sitting at the location you've chosen for your work puts you in control, putting the leading expert in the world on the job.

Try to keep this area pristine, uncontaminated by other parts of your life. If you have to use the kitchen table, use a corner that you normally don't use, or sit at a different place. At a minimum, turn your chair at a different angle from that which you sit when you eat. That separation from other parts of your life triggers the idea that you are there to work on your success story.

Regardless of how you furnish or light your special workspace, remember that your goal is to create an environment that encourages your success. If you have a special furnishing—a desk or a lamp, for example—that feels like it was made especially for you, then keep it and use it. In her book *The Western Guide to Feng Shui,* Terah Kathryn Collins says, "One of the most powerful actions you can take is to live with what you love." Surround yourself in your success space with items that you love.

Maybe you've seen or heard the term TANSTAAFL (There ain't no such thing as a free lunch). This means you will pay a price for your success. This is not as ominous as it sounds. It means that you will be forced to discard something of a lower order to make room for something higher.

When most people think of the word sacrifice, they assume it means they will have to give up something. In this case the sacrifice could be to choose not to watch a movie but to engage in activities that bring you closer to your dream.

As soon as you can honestly tell yourself, "I am willing to pay the price," you move to the next level of creating a reality out of what was previously only a dream. Use your conscious mind to ask yourself the question when the opportunity arises. If you find yourself doing something nonproductive, ask yourself, "Am I paying the price?" Use that question to refocus your energy and your actions to the quest for your dream.

Earlier in the book I mentioned the importance of velocity. What's velocity? In physics, it's the rate of the change of a position. To have velocity requires both speed and direction.

Currently you may not be where you want to be. You have determined that you are going to change your position. Obviously the direction you want is up, and the speed that you want the change to occur is fast.

For our purpose, then, you achieve velocity when you are moving upward, or toward your goal, in the fastest manner possible. If you have done the work so far—established your purpose based on your values, formed a clear image in your mind of what a successful you looks like, and determined that you are willing to pay the price—you are already achieving velocity.

Besides eagerness to reach your goal, there's another reason to reach velocity as soon as possible. It's another physics term known as inertia. Inertia is the tendency of a body at rest to stay at rest.

You're suffering from inertia if you find it difficult to get out of your chair and do the things you know you should do to reach your goals. Inertia is affecting you if you simply go through the motions at your job because your career holds no joy for you. Inertia is suffering the dull, aching pain of a life that you have settled for instead of one that brings you pleasure.

Even if you have decided to make changes in your life to create a new, successful you, the forces of inertia will try to drag you down. The only way to overcome them is to do something exciting right now.

Right now is the only time you have to actually do anything. You might plan to do something in the future, or you might have done something in the past, but right now is the only time you have to take action. If you put off taking action now, then inertia will make it difficult to do what you need to do to create your future. Now is all you have.

The beginning of the process of self-improvement is always the hardest. It's been said that the rockets that took the astronauts into outer space used most of their fuel to escape the earth's pull. After the rocket had reached the vacuum of space, the earth's gravity fell away dramatically, and very little fuel was needed to keep the rocket on course.

By acting energetically now, you will be able to escape the pull of your old life and reach the point in your journey where the powers of the universe are working for you. Your aim is to reach that point as quickly as possible by attaining velocity.

The tool you'll use to reach peak velocity is what I have named the Orange Card. The Orange Card represents the ultimate secret weapon for the attainment of any goal or change you want to make in your life. It is your personal ticket to a new you, a new life, or a new whatever it is that you truly want. I have been developing and refining the Orange Card for over ten years, and it will shock and astound you with its power. It is my strong opinion that your life is going nowhere until you have properly created and placed your own Orange Card!

Profile: Michael Jordan

MICHAEL JORDAN IS CONSIDERED by many to be the best basketball player who ever lived. Besides leading the Chicago Bulls to multiple NBA championships, Jordan also became known by his endorsement deals, such as Air Jordan shoes. What many people don't know is that before he became a basketball star, Michael Jordan faced failure as a basketball player early in his life.

Jordan grew up in Wilmington, North Carolina. As a sophomore in high school, he tried out for the varsity basketball team. But at a skinny five-foot-eleven, Jordan was considered too short and too scrawny, and he was cut from the varsity team. The summer following his sophomore year, Jordan grew four inches and trained hard. The next year, he made the varsity team and began his now-famous run toward stardom in college and the NBA.

One aspect of Jordan's game that is often overlooked is his work ethic. Learned early on from his father and reinforced during his disappointment in high school, the work ethic showed itself with the extra practice time that Jordan put in after the rest of the team was gone. The early influences in this case helped create a sports legend.

Points to Remember

We all want to make a difference.

Before you do anything else, you must define your purpose.

Keep your eye on the prize.

Your values help to determine your purpose.

To clarify your purpose, create a one-sentence purpose statement for your life.

Every accomplishment is achieved in the mind first.

At first, don't worry about how you'll accomplish your goal—simply envision the goal as if already a fact.

Take an inventory of what's right about you.

To better picture your goal, find and emulate a role model.

Use the power of directed imagination to create the perfect role model.

Focused energy is a powerful tool in your quest for success.

By focusing your attention and activity on creating the image you have created, a natural law will come into play—the universal law of attraction.

When you have a specific goal in mind you must concentrate on that goal almost to the point of obsession.

Your area of concern is nearly always larger than the area of your world that is under your control.

You must form an environment that is conducive to achieving your goal.

Create a "success space."

Remember TANSTASFL (There ain't no such thing as a free lunch).

As soon as you can honestly tell yourself "I am willing to pay the price," you move to the next level of creating your new reality.

Use this process to achieve velocity (rapid movement toward your goal).

– THE ORANGE CARD SOLUTION –

> *"An apprentice may only want a hammer and a saw, but a master craftsman employs many precision tools."*
>
> — Robert L. Kruse

What is the Orange Card?

Why is language important?

How do I use the Orange Card?

How can the Orange Card help me be more successful?

Are there larger forces at work to help me succeed?

I n The Lord of the Rings, the wizard Gandalf uses his magic to aid the adventurers on their quest. Gandalf was a very powerful wizard, filled with magic. To focus his magic powers, he used his staff. The staff was a talisman, a tool that helped him perform his magic. For you to achieve your own goals, you need a tool as well. Your talisman is the Orange Card.

The Orange Card is a focal point for your energy. It is a physical manifestation of your commitment to creating the new reality that you have created in your mind. By using an actual object, you have a constant reminder of what you are striving for. The Orange Card is your purpose made physical.

We'll get into the process in a moment. For now you need to realize that the Orange Card is more than just a piece of paper. It's concrete evidence of your commitment and provides the basis for all positive change. The Orange Card facilitates the process that allows the law of attraction to work for you.

We are talking about language here. Language is the process because you are communicating with the subconscious mind. Without effective communication you cannot fully utilize the complete power that is harnessed in the subconscious mind.

Linguist Benjamin Whorf has noted that language shapes thoughts and emotions, determining one's perception of reality. John Stuart Mill said, "Language is the light of the mind." Experts in language and communication agree that words mean things. Simply put, if we use positive language on ourselves and with others, we will have positive results. If we use negative language, we will have negative results.

The Austrian philosopher Ludwig Wittgenstein felt that philosophy was not about trying to answer spiritual questions about the nature of being or the meaning of life. Instead, he believed that philosophy was a way of mastering language and using it correctly.

Human beings use language as a tool. We use it to describe things, to give and receive orders, to report events, to tell jokes—the list is almost endless. Our minds understand words in a certain way, and if we misuse language, it is almost inevitable that the purpose of the words will be misunderstood.

Remember that the subconscious mind makes the decisions and will discuss the process with the conscious mind if it feels like it. We want to use language to convince the subconscious mind that manifesting a reality out of the image you have created is the right thing to do. The correct use of language is required for this to be successful.

Cognitive psychologists have determined that if a person has heard information before, no matter how accurate it is or in what context it's being used, they will later be more likely to remember the information as true. They refer to this phenomenon as implicit memory. Test subjects believe references, saying that the information "rings a bell" or "strikes a chord." The brief conclusion is that familiarity increases credibility.

Because of this implicit memory, the language you use with yourself is important. The subconscious mind believes what it hears most often. What we want to achieve with the Orange Card is to convince the subconscious mind that the image we have created is the true reality we want.

The Orange Card carries your statement to the universe. Your statement will invoke the power of your subconscious mind and the law of attraction. The Orange Card is a tool and much more—it is the vessel that carries your aspirations and sense of purpose, fulfilling what the cosmos has deemed rightfully yours. The statement on the Orange Card is structured like this:

an expression of gratitude and pleasure

a specific action

a specific deadline

an expression of willingness to pay the price

a reinforcement of the image of your new reality

An example might be "I am now happy and thankful that I will have a net worth of one million dollars by January 1, _____. In exchange, I will work extra hours to grow my business. I now clearly see myself performing the steps and the planning needed to achieve this." Your card should be carried with you at all times, and read several times a day.

Let's break the success statement down into its components.

An Expression of Gratitude and Pleasure

JACK BOLAND ONCE WROTE in his book *And That's the Way It Really Is!,* "What you think about expands, and a grateful attitude clears the way for more good to enter your life." Sincere gratitude is an expression of acceptance. Think about every memorable acceptance speech given by an award winner—they thank a lot of people.

We must work in harmony with the law of attraction if we are to receive what it offers. We must adopt a sincerely receptive attitude; otherwise, we are trying to trick or manipulate a natural law, which will always fail. To succeed, we must embrace the concept that we humbly accept what the universe is willing to give us.

We start the Orange Card success statement with gratitude because we want to express that thought forcefully. The gratitude statement imprints itself on our subconscious mind until we become the statement. The energy that comes from our attitude emits from us and connects with the powerful energies in the universe. We reach that state of harmony and acceptance, and we are receptive to what is available to us.

Gratitude also expresses humility. Although we control our actions, and intelligent actions control our results, we also must understand that we work in alignment with larger, universal laws that determine how our actions will be returned to us. Only by striving for harmony with these laws by displaying true humility will we be able to achieve the desired results.

We express pleasure immediately after gratitude. While the gratitude will be broadcast from us to the universe, the pleasure statement emphasizes to the subconscious mind the decision it is required to make. The pleasure statement gives us control over how we will feel when the realization of our dream comes true.

In this case we are using the principle of implicit memory to convince our subconscious mind of the pleasure we will derive from realizing the truth of our image. Using conscious thought, we are helping the subconscious mind to choose to react with pleasure.

Your Action Statement

THE ACTION STATEMENT EMPHASIZES that you are in control of your fate. You choose to do, be, or have whatever you have set your sights on. By deciding that you are going to take action, you tell your subconscious mind, and the universe, that you are deserving of whatever rewards come your way.

Your action statement also determines that the image you have created is not static. The sense of movement and activity shows that what you have imagined is not the end, but, a step toward even more riches.

The Deadline

WE ALL HAVE VAGUE aspirations—things it would be nice to do. Maybe you'd like to go on a tropical vacation someday. That's daydreaming. You're not a daydreamer anymore. You are taking control of your life, and your success will come, not someday, but at a specific time and day of your choice.

Human beings are, by nature, lazy creatures. If you are going to be the most successful you possible, then your efforts and plans call for a sense of urgency. Each of us has a limited amount of time on the planet, and only by using your time—and setting deadlines—can you achieve your desires. By putting a deadline in your success statement, you tell your subconscious, "Let's make achieving this goal a priority."

Paying the Price

WHEN IT COMES TO achievement, Mike Ferry says, "How bad do you want it? And what price are you willing to pay to get it?" We discussed earlier that there is always a price to pay for success. Without a willingness to pay the price you must pay to achieve your dreams, you are merely indulging in fantasy. Fantasizing is a necessary, but lower, order of thought. You have moved beyond that phase and understand that mature thought demands you pay a price for your success.

Having determined that you are willing to pay the price, you must convince your subconscious mind that any price you pay for your success will be worth it. In other words, the reward will far outweigh any temporary pain you feel.

Reinforcement of Your New Reality

ONE FINAL STEP TOPS off your success statement—you emphasize to your subconscious mind that you clearly envision your success. The image you have created through this process has no fuzzy lines and no blank spaces. You are the artist and the architect of your dream. You leave no doubt that the image you have envisioned is so complete that it is real. At this point your subconscious mind accepts the image as reality.

The Orange Card, with your success statement, provides the basis for any positive improvement. Used in accordance with natural laws such as the universal law of attraction, your success is assured. More than just a piece of paper, your Orange Card is a personal statement that your winning is no longer in doubt—it's just a matter of time.

I carry mine with me every day. You should carry yours with you too, if you are serious about positive change in your life. I know you are.

Profile: Roger Bannister

ROGER BANNISTER WAS BORN in Middlesex, England, and attended school in a suburb of London. He showed an early interest in and aptitude for running. Coming from a working class family, an expensive university education seemed out of reach for the youngster. However, he resolved at a young age to win a place at one of the top universities and study medicine.

Bannister's family moved to Bath at the beginning of World War II. There his intensity and studiousness kept him from being popular with the other children. But he had a chance to develop his track skills by running to and from school each day, and his success in track finally won him acceptance. More importantly, he won a scholarship to Oxford University.

At Oxford, Bannister continued to impress with his skills, and it was a shock to many when he declined to compete in the 1948 Olympics. He thought it more important to further develop his running skills and concentrate on his medical studies.

In 1951, he was the English champion in the mile and the European champion in the 1500 meters, and he felt ready to compete in the 1952 Helsinki Olympics. Scheduling conflicts forced him to compete in the two events without much of a rest in between, and he finished well down in the standings. The British press scorned him because of his unusual coaching and training techniques.

Bannister resolved to win back their respect by breaking the four-minute mile—something no human being had ever done. At the same time, he continued his medical studies, leaving him only forty-five minutes a day to train. He had seen his times improve gradually over the years, and he believed that slow and steady improvement would help him break the record.

On May 6, 1954, he had the chance to show what he could do. Working with teammates to help pace himself, he completed the mile in 3:59:04—the fastest mile ever run by a human being. At age twenty-five, Bannister had accomplished what was previously considered impossible. Within a month, another runner had broken the impossible four-minute mark, and since his initial run, the mark has been broken many times.

Roger Bannister went on to run other races with great success before retiring from competition and devoting himself to medicine. He has enjoyed a distinguished career as a physician since.

Bannister's greatest success was in showing other runners what was possible. Serving as a role model for runners was never his intention, but he nevertheless showed what was possible for a runner who focused on beating a particular time. With his first 3:59:04 mile, Roger Bannister set a mark that runners have aspired to reach ever since.

Points to Remember

The Orange Card is a focal point for your energy.

Language is the process.

Your success statement contains an expression of gratitude and pleasure, a specific action, a deadline, an expression of willingness to pay the price, and a reinforcement of the image of your new reality.

When the Orange Card is used in accordance with natural laws, such as the universal law of attraction, your success is assured.

Chapter Five

The Orange Card
and Love

–THE ORANGE CARD
AND LOVE–

"One word frees us of all the weight and pain of life—that word is love."

— Sophocles

What exactly do we mean by "relationship?"

What's so important about a first impression?

Can I make myself more appealing?

Are there different kinds of love?

What's the secret to successful relationships?

The English poet John Donne wrote that "no man is an island, entire unto himself." Every person is connected to other people. Our relationships with other people are a large part of what define us as human beings.

Most of us engage in our relationships with others haphazardly. Our family, of course, is a major part of our lives over which we have little choice. But we become friends with those we attend school with or with people we work with. For most of us, those people who we are thrown together with become the most important and vital people in our lives.

At this point, however, you are beginning to understand that we control our lives through the choices we make. The way we choose our relationships—both with whom we will interact and how we will interact—is the way we control that aspect of our lives. Using the Orange Card, we can form meaningful relationships with the people that we choose, rather than those with whom we are we are simply thrown together.

What is a relationship? By definition, it's any interaction between two people. A nod to a stranger you pass on the sidewalk constitutes a relationship. For the purposes of this chapter, though, we'll restrict our working definition of relationship to romantic interactions, or at least to a level of affection that means more than friends.

This level of affection is significant in that most of us do not fall in love with a person we have just met. Love at first sight is a romantic notion and certainly happens on occasion. For most of us, love and romance blossom from a relationship that has been cultivated at a less-intense level of friendship or affection. Relationships operate in different phases and at different levels, and love and romance typically move through preliminary levels first.

Although love may not happen at first sight, attraction certainly does. In fact, psychologists have said that an impression is formed within three seconds of meeting someone new. But wait, you say, that's not fair. Shouldn't we get to know someone first before we form an impression? If you find yourself saying this, then you're arguing with natural laws.

One theory is that early man had to be able to develop a quick impression of a situation to survive. Getting to know someone wasn't an option. Only the ones who cultivated the ability to assess another person quickly survived.

In a perfect world, we would all get to know everyone before we formed an opinion. Because the world is imperfect, however, we can move forward with the knowledge that quick first impressions, accurate or not, will occur.

Why is the impression so quick? Researchers say that upon meeting someone new, our brains immediately gather the different signals being given off by that person and form a snapshot. The image is communicated to the subconscious mind where an opinion is formed. This is simply another example of how our perfect brains work. The subconscious mind communicates in images, and first impressions fit smoothly into that system.

Psychology uses a term called imprinting. Imprinting is a rapid judgment based on a first impression, regardless of how accurate or correct that opinion is. The strength of the opinion is difficult, and sometimes impossible, to change. In nature, a baby animal bonds to the first creature it sees, which is usually its mother. This instinct has been illustrated in movies by having, for example, a flock of baby geese bond to a human who then has to teach them how to fly.

Human beings operate on a higher level, of course, and most first impressions can be changed over a period of time. Nonetheless, implementing such a change is very difficult, and time and interaction are required to do it.

Book publishers and sellers know that readers actually do choose a book by its cover. Thousands of dollars are spent to make a book's cover appealing to the proper group of readers. When a book buyer is confronted with thousands of titles on bookstore shelves, publishers use every resource they can to gain the buyer's attention.

If those in charge of marketing to the rest of us work hard to create a great first impression, doesn't it make sense that we should use the same principle in cultivating our relationships?

It's been said before, but it bears repeating—you don't get a second chance to make a first impression. In the time it takes you to think about it, the subconscious mind has already decided. When meeting someone new, the way you dress, your posture, your attitude, and a multitude of other factors combine to form the image that the other person uses to judge you. This is so important that I have incorporated it as a training module at many of my seminars.

If the first impression is positive, then the relationship can build and grow on that judgment. If the first impression is negative, then the second impression will essentially be damage control. You'll be in the position of trying to rebuild the relationship with broken parts.

At the beginning of the book, I mentioned the Power Smile that charismatic people seem to always have. Wouldn't it be great to have that kind of tool working for you when you meet people?

Professor of psychology Paul Ekman says that a smile is visible from thirty meters away. Your smile can be a billboard for you and attract people to you. A smile makes you look approachable. The person seeing you decides that they are likely to get a positive reception if they seek you out, and it makes them want to reciprocate.

People interpret a smile as "something good is happening, and I feel good because of this." Again, this all works on the subconscious level, but people recognize that for some reason, they feel good when they're around you.

What are the qualities of the Power Smile? Good hygiene, obviously. Although the Power Smile is not created in a dentist's chair. Proper care is a requirement for creating the impression you want to have on people.

More important, though, is conveying the impression that you are confident and happy. Most people are attracted to confidence, and everyone aspires to be more confident. You can tell when a person is confident because he smiles fully, without concern. The smile is not a part of the process of having confidence, it's the result of having confidence. And at this point, your confidence is riding high because you have done the work with the Orange Card and your purpose statement. You are in sync with the universe.

As mentioned earlier, people associate a happy smile with good feelings. Notice how a person begins to smile when he approaches someone else who is smiling. The combination of happiness and confidence defines a winner. When you feel happy and confident, you won't have trouble communicating that with other people. People recognize a winner when they see one.

Each of us is the center of our own universe. We are involved in our own concerns, our own problems, and how we are going to get through our day. We look for the best bargains when we shop and think about the things that interest us.

So when someone expresses interest in us, they suddenly become more attractive. Applying that principle in your relationships can open doors for you. Public speakers and salespeople know that the people they're talking to have one overriding concern—what's in it for me?

Having a genuine interest in other people makes them much more receptive to you. By being attentive to the interests and needs of another person, the law of attraction begins to take effect. A generosity of spirit on your part attracts the generosity of the universe to you.

This is something that can't be faked. For this natural law to work for you, your interest in the other person has to be heartfelt and genuine. Your impulse might be to concern yourself with involving the other person in your own interests and desires. If you resist this urge, and become involved with the other person's world, you will soon find that they will reciprocate.

It is not possible to control how other people react to you. There are simply too many variables outside your control that can affect their reaction. Having said that, you can influence the way people respond to you. The main factor in the impact you can have on their response is your self-image. How do you see yourself?

How you view yourself is apparent to other people. The subconscious mind instantly gathers information and processes it into an opinion. If you view yourself as a winner, other people will interact with you with that in mind. They will be more receptive to your ideas, open to your suggestions, and act in such a way that they think will make you happy.

When you convey a winning image, people will emulate you. We naturally look for common characteristics with those around us. As this affinity grows, so does the bond between people. If you want to influence people around you, try to find characteristics you have in common.

Also remember that people respond to positive vibrations. Even if they can't identify it, they will feel good about being around you when you maintain and convey a positive outlook. Negativity is destructive, but positive thinking is always attractive.

Entire books have been devoted to the study of body language and all its intricacies. For full training on the subject of body language, consult the library or the Internet. This chapter can't be all-inclusive with details on all the aspects of body language and physical communication, but we can touch on some principles.

First, be observant. You can't expect to pick up on clues other people are giving you if you don't pay attention. Some gestures are so subtle that they are easy to miss if you don't watch closely.

Second, be genuine in your own gestures. You might be tempted to try to communicate a false message with learned body language. Such a fraudulent approach is manipulative and runs counter to the natural laws with which we want to work in harmony. However, after learning a bit about body language, if a movement or gesture feels comfortable and genuine, then use it in an appropriate way at the proper time.

Although manipulative behavior is dishonest, being able to express your own thoughts and feelings using your body simply adds a level of communication to your connection with other people. Think of it as learning a second language.

It's important that you have an idea of the basics of body language. Besides being able to communicate better, you want to make sure that you're not sending out the wrong signals.

There are various romantic signals that can be given and received. Although not comprehensive, the following tips are a few things that you can watch for.

Preening Behavior

HAVE YOU EVER WATCHED a peacock spread out its tail feathers? It's trying to make itself look more attractive. Animals will call attention to themselves with different behaviors, often by preening or performing maintenance tasks on themselves.

When someone is attracted to you, they may make preening gestures. A person with long hair may toss it constantly, as though to reveal the face. A man may straighten his tie.

Leaning

AS AMERICANS, WE TAKE our space very seriously. We each have a bubble around us that we're very protective of. If someone invades the bubble, we become anxious. However, as counter-intuitive as it may seem, when we are talking to someone, if the listener leans forward to become closer to us, it's a sign that they are in agreement. Use space wisely when interacting with another person, and be aware of what message you are communicating.

Eye Contact

TOO MUCH EYE CONTACT becomes a stare, which can be interpreted as threatening. But if someone's gaze lingers on you a bit longer than normal, it's an indication that they might be attracted to you. Use this information to silently communicate your attraction to another person who interests you.

Smile

OF COURSE, THE BEST body language message of all—smile.

When it comes to relationships, we often have an either-or mentality. Either we can have a lot of lower-quality relationships, or we can have a few high-quality relationships. This is just old-fashioned, poorly-programmed thinking. There is no reason that we can't have high-quality relationships with everyone we know. When it comes to relationships, you can have both quality and quantity.

This does not mean that everyone you know will love you or even like you. You are not responsible for their poor programming or the subconscious loads of misinformation that they carry around because of that programming. What you can do is present an attractive package to another person and conduct yourself in a pleasant, confident way. To repeat an earlier point, you can influence another person's reaction to you, but they are not robots with buttons that you can press to get the response you want every time. Absolute control is neither desirable nor possible.

That having been said, there are different levels of relationships, and you can make sure that each level is as high quality as possible. Using the Orange Card and the principles surrounding it, you can make yourself as attractive as possible at every level and to every person with whom you interact. Let's take a quick look at the various levels of relationship.

Business/Casual

AT THE BUSINESS OR casual level you know the person's name and maybe not much more. You deal with them either at work or in another environment and don't necessarily need to reveal much about yourself. With these people, you can project an image of confident, friendly professionalism. By following the principles of the Orange Card, you are the proverbial "man with a mission," and they know it. They can tell by the way you interact with those who you know only casually.

A common reaction among people who know you only casual may be, "I don't know him or her very well, but I'd like to get to know them better." If it's a business relationship, you'll find that people will want to do business with you, and they won't really know why. Of course, you know that it's their subconscious mind making the decision for them.

If it's a non-business relationship, people will want to associate with you more. They may find excuses to show up where you are or participate in some of the same activities. Your opinion will mean more to them.

What is happening is that as you become more attuned to the vibrations of the universe, you emit an energy that communicates success. People will begin to tune in to your vibrations, and the more they do that, the more appealing spending time with you becomes.

Friendship

SOME OF THE PEOPLE who you know casually may progress to friends. It's at this point that your Orange Card really has an effect. Because they know more about you, they will see that you are on a path to success. It's a law of nature that people want to associate with winners.

When you have found your purpose in life, and you are fulfilling it, your behavior is shouting "Winner!" to everyone you associate with. Because you have a feeling of gratitude and pleasure, you are generous with praise and help for others. The spirit of giving and generosity permeates everything you do.

I'm not necessarily talking about being generous with your money, although that might occasionally come into play. I'm talking about being able to be with another person in the now, focused on that person and ignoring trivial distractions. Your own self-assuredness makes it possible for you to be interested in what the other person is saying.

Lovers

SOME OF THE PEOPLE will progress to the highest level of romantic love or what the Bible calls agape love. Just as with the other levels, your knowledge and fulfillment of your life purpose will make you attractive to others on more than just a surface level. As you become a higher-quality person, you will enjoy higher-quality relationships.

The main principle to keep in mind is to make every relationship as productive as you can. You want the other person to get as much out of the relationship as you do. In every interaction you want to think win-win. Focus as much on what you give as on what you can get. By giving all you have to every relationship, you are invoking the law of reciprocation, which will ensure that you get the results that you want. It has been said for years that you can have pretty much anything you want in life if you help other people get what they want.

How does the Orange Card come into play in your relationships? It is the same way as mentioned in previous chapters—you envision the result you want and the purpose you have for your relationships. In this case, however, instead of determining that you will achieve a certain level of compensation, you express the confidence that you will enjoy a particular level of relationship.

Once again you have to use your vision to clearly identify what a loving, close relationship will look like to you. You can use role models in your own life or create your own role models of how the relationship will appear. Imagine what your perfect partner would look like. Picture how you will interact with him or her. Think of the pleasure the relationship will give you and the gratitude you will feel for the opportunity to have such a bond.

At this point, the image should be clear, and you should form your Orange Card statement as though the situation were already in existence.

An example of a successful Orange Card statement might be "I am now happy and grateful that I will be involved in a close, loving, and rewarding relationship by January 1, _____. In exchange, I will act as a loving, caring person and be thoughtful of others. I now clearly see myself performing the steps and planning to achieve this."

Once again you have to use your vision to clearly identify what a loving, close relationship will look like to you.

With this example, you can see how the Orange Card can be used in every part of your life. We are defined by our relationships, and by focusing your energies on the quality of your relationships, you will find that the quantity of rewarding relationships will increase. You will find that you appear more attractive to other people because of the spiritual growth you experience, and you become the type of person that deserves love and affection.

As you can tell, what might appear to be an external exercise—looking more appealing to other people—is really a very important internal exercise, spiritual exercise. It is more of a *becoming* than an *appearing*. Although surface factors such as dress and physical appearance are very important, they are secondary to the importance of being the type of person who earns and deserves the love of others.

One of the best pieces of advice I ever received came from the father of a good friend. He said, "Make yourself the man you know you should be, and you will attract the right people to you."

Profile: Napoleon Hill

NAPOLEON HILL, THE FOUNDER of "the science of success," started humbly. He was born in a one-room cabin in Virginia in 1883. His mother died when he was young, and Hill became a rebellious boy. He managed to get a job at age thirteen as a mountain reporter for a local, small-town newspaper, and thus began his writing career.

Hill spent several years as a reporter, and used the earnings to finance his way through law school, eventually becoming an attorney as well as a journalist. One of his assignments was to write a series of articles on successful men, and his greatest opportunity came when he was asked to interview steel magnate Andrew Carnegie.

After developing a relationship with Carnegie, Hill was commissioned by the millionaire to interview hundreds of successful people to determine if there was a "success formula" that the average person could apply to his or her life. As a result of this assignment, Hill was able to interview giants in American industry, including Thomas Edison, Henry Ford, Alexander Graham Bell, Charles Schwab, Theodore Roosevelt, William Jennings Bryan, George Eastman, William Howard Taft, Woodrow Wilson, John D. Rockefeller, and many more.

Drawing on the thoughts, experiences, and advice of a multitude of tycoons—many of them self-made—and with the help of Carnegie, Hill was able to construct a philosophy of success that resulted in his self-help masterpiece, *Think and Grow Rich*. The book took over twenty years to write, but since its publication, it has sold more than seven million copies and helped countless people achieve success.

Napoleon Hill influenced the self-improvement field more than any other person in history. Success authors, such as W. Clement Stone and Og Mandino, owe their starts to Hill's influence. *Think and Grow Rich* is considered the cornerstone of self-improvement literature.

All of this came from the efforts of a boy born in a one-room cabin in Virginia. It was truly a remarkable journey for Napoleon Hill, exemplifying what was perhaps his most famous quote: "Anything the mind of man can conceive and believe, man can achieve."

Points to Remember

Our relationships with other people define who we are as human beings.

Looking at your friends is like looking in the mirror.

We control the romantic aspect of our lives by how we choose our relationships.

Relationships operate in different phases and at different levels, and love and romance typically move through preliminary levels first.

First impressions are formed within the first three seconds of meeting someone new.

It's difficult to change a first impression.

A genuine, happy smile attracts people and makes them want to approach you.

When you interact with another person, their main interest is WIIFM—"What's in it for me?"

Knowledge of body language is necessary to avoid sending out the wrong signals as well as interpreting the signals other people are sending.

Only 7 percent of communication is the words—38 percent is your voice, and 55 percent is your appearance.

It's possible to have both quality and quantity in your relationships. Focus on the quality, and the quantity will grow.

There are different levels of relationships, and you can make sure that each level is as high quality as possible.

In every interaction with other people, think win-win.

In relationships, focus as much on what you can give as what you can get.

When you give all you have to every relationship, the law of reciprocation ensures that you get all you desire.

Looking more appealing to other people is a very internal, spiritual exercise. It is more of a becoming than an appearing.

Surface factors, such as dress and physical appearance, are secondary to the importance of being the type of person who earns and deserves the love of others.

Chapter Six

The Orange Card
and Your Health

—THE ORANGE CARD AND YOUR HEALTH—

"As I see it, every day you do one of two things: build health or produce disease in yourself."

— Adelle Davis

Is there a connection between mind and body?

What's the definition of good health?

Can we heal our body with our mind?

What are the components of good health?

How important is diet?

I s there a connection between the mind and the body? That question has been asked by philosophers since the time of Aristotle. The sixteenth-century French philosopher Rene Descartes put his view on it simply—"Cogito, ergo sum" (I think, therefore I am). There's no doubt that the mind and the body have some sort of connection.

Medical researchers certainly think so. When they test a new drug, they always have two groups—the test group and the control group. One group takes the drug being tested, and the other takes a placebo. At a certain stage in development and testing, they use a double-blind methodology, meaning neither the researchers nor the patients know which group is taking which treatment.

What researchers have found is that sometimes both groups improve. In 1955, researcher H. K. Beecher published a paper in which he concluded that an average of 32 percent of patients responded to placebo treatments. The word placebo comes from Latin, and it means "I shall be pleasing." The important question to ask is not "Why are placebos so effective," but "Why do placebos work at all?"

Of course, the causes of some ailments are physical in nature and can't be cured with an empty pill. But scientific research has proven that there is a definite connection between the way the mind works and the physical condition and health of the body.

One of the ways the mind affects the body's physical state is to cause the onset of poor health habits. Depression, sadness, anger, and any other negative emotions can lead us to lean on crutches such as alcohol, drugs, or food. Although any of these habits may not be destructive in small amounts for a brief period of time, the emotions that lead to dependence on them impair our judgment. Impaired judgment leads to excessive use and abuse.

The seductive nature of these habits is part of the danger. A patient of mine wanted to quit smoking cigarettes, so he went to a stop-smoking workshop. There he learned about the nature of cigarettes—the cost, the health risks, etc. Additionally, he discovered that he had made his cigarette his best friend. When he was sad, he smoked a cigarette. When he was happy, he smoked a cigarette. When he celebrated, he smoked a cigarette.

The man successfully stopped smoking, and the final step in his process was to have a funeral for his last cigarette. He took the final puff, literally said good-bye, and buried the cigarette butt in his back yard. He was paying his last respects to a lost friend. The insidious nature of bad habits is that they cloak themselves in emotions that make the user feel good—at least temporarily.

That's the deceptive nature of these habits. They may make you feel good or special at the beginning, but in the end, they all take away from you. If a person could evaluate the positives and negatives as they went along, they would see where the habit had crossed over from being enjoyable to being destructive, dangerous, and harmful to their physical health.

Drug abuse is a fairly straightforward example of how the mind can affect the body—impaired judgment leading to poor decisions leading to harmful habits. Few, if any, people start a drug habit with the intention of becoming addicted. They may feel weak or in pain and look for something, anything, to help make the pain go away. The drugs satisfy a craving for relief. In other ways, the connection can be a little more mysterious.

Norman Cousins was the editor for *Saturday Review* magazine. He suffered from a very serious and painful spine disease that was getting progressively worse. One doctor estimated that Norman had a one in five hundred chance to survive. The medical treatments the doctors were providing were having little effect.

Cousins decided to take his treatment into his own hands. He checked out of the hospital and into a hotel. Once there, he started taking massive doses of vitamin C. He had been under some stress and felt that stress contributed to his condition. He thought if negative emotions can cause negative physical symptoms, then could positive emotions have positive effects on the body?

Cousins began to watch comedies—Marx Brothers movies and episodes of *Candid Camera*. He later recalled: "I found that ten minutes of belly laughter gave me an hour of pain-free sleep." Slowly, he began to improve. He enjoyed a complete recovery and lived another twenty-five years.

Clearly something beyond the norm went on with Norman Cousins. When traditional medicine, with all its science and research, couldn't help him, his mind took control and healed his body. He made conscious decisions on what to do and allowed positive energy to do its work with him.

When we feel fear or excitement, epinephrine is secreted by the adrenal gland. Our heart rate increases, our pupils dilate, and our body prepares for fight or flight. All of these physical reactions are provoked by an emotion. That leaves little doubt that the mind can have profound effects on the body.

Again, we see that there is a definite connection between the body's condition and mental function.

Can the body affect the mind? Vince Lombardi thought so. After years of coaching in the NFL and observing professional-caliber athletes under extreme physical duress, he commented, "Fatigue makes cowards of us all." He knew that when his players got tired in the fourth quarter of a game that their will to win fell off considerably. Using his observations as a basis, he emphasized conditioning for his teams and went on to win NFL championships.

Chronic fatigue syndrome—a physical condition—has several physical indications, but symptoms can also include problems with concentration and short-term memory. Sufferers may also experience difficulties in remembering the right word to express their thoughts, inability to comprehend what someone else is saying or calculate numbers, or impairment of reasoning.

I had a patient once who came to me for back pain. I performed an evaluation and took an X-ray. I then told him to come back the next day for my opinion. When he came back the next day, he said, "Dr. Robson, I don't know what you did yesterday, but I feel 100 percent better today!" I found this quite interesting since I hadn't rendered any treatment yet—or had I?

Again, we see that there is a definite connection between the body's condition and mental function. The channel that connects the mind and body is a two-way street. When we are sick, in pain or distress, or fatigued or sleepy, the mind is not able to function at its highest levels. Memory is affected as is alertness and reaction time—all high-level functions that are necessary for survival. The body's condition determines the mind's condition.

The body's effect on the mind can also be beneficial. When a person is in good health, physically fit, and getting enough rest and fresh air, he is more mentally alert than someone who is sedentary and hardly goes outside. Positive physical health promotes good thinking, feelings, and emotions.

It's accepted that negative emotions affect the body. Stress causes high blood pressure and ulcers. Anxiety can cause muscle pain and stomach problems. Even more, though, there are observable signs that negative thoughts are affecting the body. Think about some of the clichés that movies use for a nervous or anxious person—bitten fingernails, rashes on the skin, and sores around the mouth. Those stereotypes would not be useful for movie writers if they weren't based on truth.

The list of negative emotions is well known. The historical seven deadly sins are based on negative emotions—lust, gluttony, greed, sloth, anger, envy, and vanity. Sadness and guilt can be added as part of modern man's emotional burdens. Although not comprehensive, this list represents some of the major negative feelings that can manifest themselves as physical problems.

Besides emotions, certain mental activities can cause problems. Worry is a huge problem in our modern world. We are bombarded with information, very little of it pleasant. The headlines scream out the terrible things going on in the world. Americans worry about a huge number of unlikely events, convinced that these disasters are going to happen.

Part of the problem is that our area of concern—those events that cause anxiety and affect us emotionally—has expanded rapidly with the advent of twenty-four-hour news channels and the Internet. Although this flood of information has grown due to technology, our area of control—those events over which we exert a direct influence—has not benefited from the same technology.

In a test conducted recently, researchers at Louisiana State University found that the lack of control by the test subjects increased their belief that a negative future event would happen. In other words, the more control the subjects felt they had, the less they worried about disasters. Is it any wonder that worry and anxiety are major sources of stress in our out-of-control, information-packed society?

Additionally, many people dwell on negative thoughts. Although it's natural to have occasional thoughts about unpleasant situations, to linger unnecessarily on something that makes you feel bad is neither healthy nor wise. We normally call such people pessimists, but when negative thinking starts affecting the quality of a person's life, common descriptions are no longer accurate—the habit of dwelling on the negative aspects of life has become pathological.

If we are looking for excellence in every area of our lives, how do we go about achieving excellent physical and mental health? For that matter, how do you define excellent health?

Physically, a few simple conditions would apply. Excellent health would mean a lack of disease or illness, plus the ability to physically perform whatever tasks we ask our bodies to do. As we saw from Norman Cousins' story, your state of mind can help your body heal itself. What if you used that positive state of mind to increase your level of health or fitness to extraordinary levels? When it comes to your physical health, you should strive not just for health, but for robust health.

If you're looking to be healthy, essentially you mean free from disease. Your aim should be to achieve a state of health where not only are you disease-free, but you are also disease-resistant. An increased immunity to diseases is possible by using and controlling your mental state. Just as depression can lower your immunity to diseases, you want to use your positive emotions to raise your resistance to disease and infection.

Disease is a condition in which the body's normal functions have been disrupted. This can be caused by a virus or bacteria, or through deteriorating conditions due to abuse of the body's systems through the use of alcohol, drugs, tobacco, or other harmful chemicals. Disease is also present when the body has been subjected to "luxury abuse"—excess food, usually of a harmful nature, combined with inactivity and lack of exercise. A person in such shape is just as ill as the person with a virus. We simply choose to call it "good living" in our society. If we realized the true effects of our modern lifestyles, we might choose to rename the condition.

Physical fitness, for our purposes, means that your body will be able to physically perform the duties that you ask of it. If your friends want to play a game of basketball, or your child needs to practice soccer, or you need to carry your child up a flight of stairs, you'll be able. Your body should not prevent you from enjoying your life.

Fitness intersects with health in some places—for instance, aerobic exercise helps prevent cardiovascular disease, and resistance training can help prevent osteoporosis. But essentially health refers to the absence of disease, while fitness refers to the functioning ability of the body.

THERE ARE FIVE COMPONENTS TO PHYSICAL FITNESS:

cardiovascular fitness

strength

flexibility

agility

your body mass index (BMI)

CARDIOVASCULAR FITNESS REFERS TO your heart's ability to pump blood. Blood carries oxygen from the lungs to the rest of the body and then circulates back to pick up more oxygen. The body's muscles and organs utilize oxygen in their various functions. (The following descriptions are for information only. Consult your doctor before starting any exercise program.)

Aerobic exercise—any exercise that makes you pant for breath—is an excellent way to improve your cardiovascular fitness. Experts recommend at least thirty minutes of aerobic exercise a day to achieve the best results. This exercise improves the heart's ability to pump blood as well as helps clear out the veins and arteries that carry the blood.

Strength refers to the ability of your muscles to exert power. We need strength throughout our day—from a construction worker lifting bags of cement to a mother carrying a toddler up a flight of stairs. With today's technology reducing the amount of physical labor most of us perform in our jobs, we need to build our strength so it'll be available when we need it.

Most experts agree that resistance training is the best way to build strength. Whether it's lifting heavy weights at a gym or doing pushups at home, muscles perform better when they're used regularly.

Some women worry that resistance training will make them big and muscular, but for most women that's not a concern. Muscle size depends on the amount of work you do and the presence of the male hormone testosterone. Most women don't have enough testosterone in their bodies to make their muscles grow to an abnormal size.

However, men and women both can get stronger with regular resistance training. The key is to put real effort into your workout. Muscle fibers rupture when they are pushed to the maximum limit. Over the next forty-eight hours, those fibers repair themselves, and the repaired muscle is then stronger than it was before—thus the commonly misunderstood phrase "no pain, no gain."

Flexibility is the body's ability to bend, twist, and move smoothly. Again, our sedentary lifestyles and growing obesity have rendered us almost inflexible. For many people, it's difficult to bend over and pick up a penny off the ground.

We need increased flexibility to avoid injury. If you're at your desk at work and someone asks you for a particular file, you may have to twist to reach the folder. Such a move can cause tremendous pain if you have not worked to increase your flexibility.

Slow, easy stretching exercises are the best way to increase the body's flexibility. Certain styles of yoga focus on making the body more supple and flexible. Unlike resistance training, while stretching, you do not want to push too hard. Gradually increase your stretch until you feel discomfort, then ease back.

Being flexible will help you move more smoothly and fluidly. You'll probably hear comments about how graceful you are. Twisting and bending will be easier for you if your muscles and connective tissues have been developed so that you achieve maximum flexibility.

Agility is the ability to move quickly from one place to another, often in an unexpected direction. Gymnasts use agility, of course, but if you've ever had to dodge someone or something on a crowded sidewalk, then you know how important agility can be in everyday life.

Agility is developed through drills and exercises that emphasize short, sudden changes in direction. Agility is sometimes described as a combination of power and flexibility. Developing those two physical aspects can help increase agility.

My secret weapon in the area of physical training has been kettlebells (sometimes called Russian kettlebells). A kettlebell is basically a cannonball with a handle. They come in a variety of weights and originated in Russia. They are the official training tool of the Russian military. Due to the kettleball's power and versatility, they are at nearly all U.S. military installations and have even been seen on Air Force One.

Brad Nelson—personal trainer, performance specialist, and nationally recognized kettlebell instructor—says, "A kettlebell's off-centered weight allows for strength, cardio, and flexibility to be trained simultaneously in a way no other training tool can match. This is why kettlebells are called the ultimate hand-held gym." I completely agree and feel that well instructed kettlebell training makes most conventional weight training obsolete. Try it, and you will likely be just as impressed.

Body mass index (BMI) is a trait of the body reflecting the percentage of body fat to lean muscle mass. A lower body fat percentage compared to the overall body composition is—to a degree—considered healthier. Although, a person can actually have too little body fat, which has its own accompanying problems. But most of us don't have to worry about that. For most adults, a healthy BMI will be in the range of 18.5 percent to 24.9 percent. (This range is an estimate only, and healthy individuals can have a BMI outside this range. Consult your doctor to find out what a healthy BMI would be for you.)

The BMI can be aligned into a healthy range by reducing body fat and increasing lean muscle mass. Body fat can be reduced with extended cardiovascular or aerobic exercise. That's why marathon runners are usually so thin—they have very little body fat. Increasing muscle mass involves resistance training to increase density and size of muscles.

BMI is more of a result of the other habits than from exercise itself. Nevertheless, when considering the different characteristics of physical fitness, it's something that must be kept in mind. We can't achieve great physical fitness if we don't consider how to combat obesity and achieve a healthy BMI.

MENTAL HEALTH IS REFLECTED more in our mind's function. Clear decision-making, appropriate knowledge, and discipline are aspects of mental health. Good relationships with other people are usually a sign of good mental health. It's difficult to pinpoint specific traits that comprise mental health because of the wide variety and diversity reflected by healthy minds.

However, we can assume some guidelines for good mental health. A mentally healthy person should, above all, have an enthusiasm for life. Unpleasant circumstances may occasionally force themselves into our lives, but there should always remain the fundamental philosophy that life should be joyous.

Of course, with the Orange Card system, we are not looking simply for answers that will help us get by. We want to live our lives not just well but joyfully. We want to be able to address any situation with quiet confidence and serenity. We want to be prepared to enjoy healthy relationships with those we care about the most.

If we want the mind and the body to work together in a smooth, coordinated way, then it almost goes without saying that we need to pursue healthy habits. In this case, the mind controls the body. We must use our conscious mind to work with the subconscious mind to help the body help itself.

Appropriate knowledge—based on age, mental development, and individual character—is important as a measure of mental health. A normally-developed person will have information about the world around them. With the wealth—or glut, depending on your point of view—of information available to us, there is no excuse for ignorance. Gathering appropriate information and applying it is a sign of a healthy, mature mind.

Good decision-making is another indicator of a healthy mind. Although we all make mistakes, it's important that we use some comparative analysis, no matter how fleeting, to make decisions. The ability to tell constructive habits from destructive habits is a sign that decisions are made in a way that is beneficial to the decision-maker. Poor decisions, such as tobacco use, drug use, or anything done to excess, can be avoided by applied use of the conscious mind.

If you have gathered information and have the ability to make a sound decision, then the other component of a healthy lifestyle is discipline. Knowledge without action is wasted. You can have all the information in the world about exercise, but unless you actually go ahead and do the workouts, you won't become one bit stronger or more physically fit. It takes discipline to deny your whims of convenience in order to earn substantial gains later.

There are basically five factors that make up the foundation for a healthy life—restful sleep, proper exercise, following a diet that is beneficial to your body, a positive mental attitude, and a sound nerve system. Although the precise nature of each of these habits will differ from person to person, some general guidelines can be suggested.

There is no cheating sleep. Most people need seven to nine hours of sleep a night. If you try to shortchange your sleep, you may feel drowsy during the day, have memory and thinking difficulties, and eventually start to suffer from diseases, such as hypertension, that can be made worse by lack of sleep.

Sleep has been found to help reinforce memories and is believed by some experts to help us process complex emotions. Also, during sleep the body secretes a hormone that helps repair and regenerate damaged tissue.

There is a period at night that I call "The Ninety Golden Minutes." This is the hour and a half from 10:30 PM to midnight. It is reported that the value and power of sleep during this time is more than that from midnight to 6 AM. Maybe this is why a nap in the afternoon is so powerful yet sleeping in doesn't seem to add much to your quality of rest.

It's clear that we should make getting enough of the right kind of sleep an important part of keeping our minds and our bodies healthy.

We discussed exercise earlier. The main principle in adopting any exercise program is to just keep doing it. Millions of people start exercising each January with the best intentions, but drop off when difficulties arise. Even if you skip a workout occasionally, keep at it. If at all possible, try to work with a trainer. A qualified trainer will provide motivation, design a program, and help you train at levels you may never reach on your own.

As for diet, we could talk about this for a while. Here are my thoughts from experiences in working with over five thousand patients:

Eat things that were alive at one time. This means eat real food that God made versus the man-made stuff we call food.

Eat lightly and simply. Eating is what you do to fuel your body—it is not a hobby or a part-time job.

Go drink a glass of water right now because there is a 90 percent chance that you are dehydrated.

Avoid these health destroyers as much as possible: sugar, salt, bad oils found in processed foods (i.e., margarine), artificial sweeteners, caffeine, soda, and cow's milk. Yes, cow's milk, for many reasons that you might want to research on your own. Many, including myself, have found rice milk to be superior to cow's milk in every way.

Avoid these health destroyers as much as possible: sugar, salt, bad oils found in processed foods (i.e., margarine), artificial sweeteners, caffeine, soda, and cow's milk.

It really isn't that difficult. Simply eat smaller meals of real food, drink more water, and avoid putting poisons in your body. I think every diet book ever written is basically trying to say this. Of course, clean eating comes from a clean mind. The body always follows the mind.

To improve your physical and mental health, it's absolutely vital to have goals. Wandering aimlessly without any sort of plan is the path to frustration and failure. With the adoption of the Orange Card program, you have already developed the habit of picturing an end result.

What kind of goal should you picture for a healthy mind and body—your mind/body connection? While you likely have goals—such as losing weight, getting more fit, or being able to sleep better—you need a larger, overall goal. That goal needs to be achieving harmony and alignment.

When your actions regarding your mind and your body work together smoothly, you have achieved harmony. It's discordant to focus entirely on the body and neglect the mind, just as it's impossible to harmoniously neglect the body and focus only on the mind. Although either option is possible, they don't meet the highest level of development that you are capable of.

Harmonious development of the mind and body has been the highest goal of leaders throughout history. From the Greek philosophers to the Japanese samurai to American presidents such as Theodore Roosevelt, we have honored those who developed the body and the mind together. We always appreciate harmony.

Alignment is the state where your actions are in accordance with your purpose. Although there are many different ways to train your body and achieve fitness, some don't go together. If you have the goal of becoming stronger or more muscular, then extensive cardiovascular exercise by itself will not achieve that goal, although you will be more physically fit. Make your goals and your actions work together. That's the only way to achieve and realize the image you create.

The last of my five factors of health is a sound nerve system. What I mean is this: what difference does it make to eat well if your stomach is only functioning at 75 percent because the nerves that power it are being shorted out by a misalignment in the vertebrae where those nerves travel?

How much will exercise really help you if you are exercising with vertebrae out of alignment, thereby grinding the joints down every time you exercise them? How effectively can you work on your goals and positive attitude if you have a headache every week caused by a misalignment in your neck that is causing nerve pressure and headaches?

What we must realize is that the body is like a race car—it needs to be tuned so it can perform better and last longer. This leads me to secret weapon number two—a good chiropractor. Without exception, a good chiropractor can be one of the best assets you and your family could ever have. Regular spinal adjustments to keep the vertebrae set in place and promote full nerve flow from the brain to the body are essential for high-level health.

Get a massage at least once a month. Consider it an investment in your health. We all realize the benefits of massage therapy. I have offered massage therapy in my office for several years. I am continually amazed at the results people achieve in their health and peace of mind with regular massage sessions.

Follow the Orange Card process. Determine your purpose regarding your physical and mental health. Form a clear image in your mind, as though watching a movie that has already been filmed. You should be looking at a smiling, confident, healthy you—a winner who is free of disease, physically fit, and comfortable with yourself. You will be happy and ready to receive the blessings that the universe has bestowed on you.

Remember to set a date. To repeat an earlier point—you set a deadline to have a way of measuring your success. Without the urgency of the date, you might be inclined to dither and think that you have all the time in the world. You don't. The only time you can take action on your goals is right now.

Consider what price you're willing to pay to reach your goals. If you've determined that half an hour of meditation is part of your goal, are you willing to turn off the television to pursue your higher priority? Are you willing to get up an hour earlier each day to work out? Each person has their own goals, but the immutable natural law still remains—there will be a price to pay as you surrender something of a lower order to achieve something of a higher order.

Finally, remember to state clearly exactly how you'll look and feel after you reach your goal. The sharper this image, the more your subconscious mind will grasp it and accept it as the reality that is to come.

Profile: Arnold Schwarzenegger

BIG, STRONG, AND MOVIE-star handsome, Arnold Schwarzenegger symbolizes physical fitness to the world. More important than his physical assets, however, are the mental toughness and intelligence that he has displayed throughout his life.

Schwarzenegger was born in Austria in 1947. As a youngster, he participated in normal games, such as soccer. It was as a teenager that he began lifting weights and developing his body. He found that the muscles in his upper body—his chest and shoulders—developed quickly when he lifted, and he enjoyed the feeling of controlling his development. As a teen he participated in local bodybuilding contests.

Despite his huge physique, there was some criticism that his development was one-dimensional and that he neglected his lower body. Schwarzenegger listened to the comments, and he realized that if he wanted to compete at higher levels, he would have to appear more balanced in his development. With this in mind, he consciously worked on the areas that he felt were weakest while still keeping his muscular upper body in shape.

Schwarzenegger worked hard to focus on his overall health and appearance, and at age twenty he became the youngest man ever to win the Mr. Universe bodybuilding title. Keeping the same mental discipline that won him his first title, he went on to win twelve more world bodybuilding titles.

Challenging both his mind and body, Schwarzenegger earned a college degree from the University of Wisconsin and became an American citizen in 1983. He parlayed his bodybuilding titles into a film career, eventually earning as much as $30 million for a single movie. During his career, he invested wisely in real estate and other endeavors, until in 2003, he had assets of approximately $68 million. In 2003, Schwarzenegger was elected governor of California, showing that he had political savvy to go along with his business acumen.

Although most people think of Schwarzenegger primarily as an example of physical strength, vitality, and muscle development, his career has proven that his mind has been as important in his success as his body. As Schwarzenegger himself said, "The mind is the limit. As long as the mind can envision the fact that you can do something, you can do it, as long as you believe 100 percent."

Points to Remember

*Mankind has always realized that there is a connection
between the mind and the body.*

*Scientific medical research has proven
that the mind affects the body.*

*Negative mental states can lead to poor
health habits, which affect the body.*

The state of the body definitely affects the state of the mind.

*The channel that connects the mind and
the body is a two-way street.*

Worry is a huge problem in our modern world.

*Thanks to modern media and technology, our area of concern has
expanded tremendously while our area of control has not.*

*The goal of excellent health requires a lack of disease,
or illness, plus the ability to physically perform whatever
tasks we ask our body to do.*

*There are five components to physical fitness: cardiovascular fitness,
strength, flexibility, agility, and body mass index (BMI).*

*A mentally healthy person should, above all,
have an enthusiasm for life.*

*If we want the mind and the body to work together in a smooth,
coordinated way, then we need to pursue healthy habits.*

*The three components of a healthy lifestyle are knowledge,
judgment, and discipline.*

Five basic habits make up the foundation for a healthy life: restful sleep, proper exercise, following a diet that is beneficial to your body, a positive attitude, and a sound nervous system.

The main principle in adopting any exercise program is to just keep doing it.

To improve your physical and mental health, it's absolutely vital to have goals.

The overall goal for a great mind/body connection is to achieve harmony and alignment.

Chapter Seven

The Orange Card
and Your Career

– THE ORANGE CARD AND YOUR CAREER –

"It's not about what career you pick. It's about how you do what you do."

— Cory Doctorow

What does my job mean to me?

How do I find a better career?

How should I handle my responsibilities?

How do I achieve an attitude of success?

What is stewardship?

Y ou are not your job.

With as many hours as most of us work, it's sometimes hard to separate our identities from our work. Whether you're self-employed or work for someone else, you put much of yourself into your labors, and the line between work-time and home-time often gets blurred. We work overtime or go in early when we are needed, and we answer the phone and help co-workers when we are off.

Regardless of what else it is, your job is primarily one thing—it's what you do for money. If you deliver letters, you're a mail carrier. If you shoe horses, you're a blacksmith. We're so used to identifying ourselves by what we do for work that we forget that the main reason we work is for a paycheck. Our self-identity becomes wrapped up in what we do for a living.

That's not all, of course, and we'll discuss the other job-related motivators later. The reason we want to separate what you do from who you are is because, for most of us, our job is one of the least thought-out life decisions we make. Surprisingly, we hurry to take a job, only to regret our decision later, sometimes for the rest of our lives.

Some people plan out their career path carefully, of course, and work the plan throughout their lives. For many, finding a job is hurried, panic-driven, and our choice is governed by lower-level factors.

Even if you are lucky enough to get a job in the field of your degree, it's usually not the one you would have chosen. Our choices are made by incidental factors, such as geography, convenience, or need for money. They are usually not made using the power of the Orange Card.

We usually take our first job close to home. If we have the luxury of more than one job offer, we take the one closest to home, all other things being equal. If you're newly married, it might mean you take a job closer to your new home. Regardless of where you wind up, the result is the same— you have used a factor to make your decision that is not always conducive to success.

Being close to home has its advantages, of course. You have the support system that you've developed over your lifetime. You know your way around the neighborhoods. You have friends to spend time with after work. As nice as those factors are, they're not the important factors that we need to use to make success-driven decisions.

Often we take the first job that's offered because we need the money. After that, it's easy to slide into a routine. Before you know it, you've devoted your entire working life to a job, a company, and maybe even a field that you never intended.

Think about it—how many college graduates are working in fields that have nothing to do with their degrees? It's common to hear of people with PhDs waiting tables or working in fast-food restaurants.

Another reason to separate who you are from your job is because companies fail. Many companies who have good people working for them fail because of poor management, the competitive climate, government regulation, or a number of other factors. You can do a great job, and the company might still fail for reasons outside your control. No one who has done their best job should feel like a failure because their company failed.

Also, your job does not define you. Who you are as a person is much more than what you do for a living. A job will use a specific set of skills that you possess. It can't utilize all the skills and talents that you possess—no job could. If anyone tries to judge you by the type of work you do (not the quality), then they miss seeing the entire picture.

A job may also be transitory. You may be in a position where you need a second income, and you decide to work an extra job. Many people augment their incomes with outside jobs. Again, how could anyone define you as a person based on the work you do, especially if it's a second job done strictly for the money?

Sometimes a particular job is taken to maintain a holding pattern. College graduates will often take a job temporarily while another job—the real job—is being prepared for them. It would be ridiculous to judge anyone based on this temporary position.

Even if you are in the job that you were meant to have and fulfilling your life's plan, you can't define your entire life based on your job. Your job is simply one role that you play in your life. Other roles—father, mother, brother, sister, son, daughter—are as much, if not more, important than what you do for employment.

Human beings are many-faceted. Even when the job is very important to them, it's simply one aspect of their life. As adults we find ourselves having to fit into a series of roles—some of our choosing and some thrust upon us. Besides your role at your job, you may have a role as a parent, brother or sister, child of older parents, coach, volunteer, or PTA member—the number of possible roles is endless.

Even in your job, you may fill different roles. As the secretary, you may be the one who handles minor tasks that the boss delegates to you—answering the phone, handling routine correspondence, or filing. At the same time, you handle an important task as the gatekeeper—the one who determines who has access to the boss's office and his time.

If you're not your job, and you don't define yourself by your job (or let the job define you,) then the question you may well ask is "What is my job?" The answer for any job—whether you work for yourself or for someone else—is to provide value. If you're self-employed, then you already know the importance of providing value to your customers. By doing that, you are on your way to the type of success you've planned for yourself.

If you work for someone else, you have to provide value to your co-workers, your managers, the company itself, and ultimately to the customers. Whatever your task, your goal must be to do more than "just enough." By being the type of person who aims for excellence instead of average, you are defining the job, rather than letting it define you.

You also must be a good steward of both your resources and your responsibilities. Resources are, by definition, finite in any endeavor, and the company's profitability, as well as its viability, depends on resources being used wisely and well. You must look to use resources, such as money, time, and energy, as efficiently and effectively as possible.

By responsibilities, I mean the actual duties you are assigned to perform. Sloppy or shoddy work hurts your reputation, your department or division, and the company. In today's work environment, good workmanship stands out. For example, isn't everyone who owns an automobile looking for a good mechanic? We have become so used to poor work that as consumers, we are constantly on the lookout for that one place, one company, or one individual who stands behind their product and their service.

Good stewardship in the workplace leads to good stewardship in your life and vice versa. Taking proper care of your world becomes a habit. For someone who aims for the highest rungs of success, nothing less than your best effort is acceptable.

Whether you work for others or with others, you fulfill a role. You are part of a team regardless of what you do. You might work in a department with other people for a large corporation, or as a self-employed individual, you may be part of a team consisting of your suppliers, customers, and your own support staff.

For your business to run smoothly, every member of the team must do his or her part. Lackadaisical performance by any one segment can cause the whole enterprise to come to a halt. Teamwork is everyone pulling together to accomplish the goal.

The company has many needs, whether in sales, production, administration, analysis, or some other function. Those needs can be met most effectively when everyone involved understands their role and fulfills their duties to the best of their ability.

All this having been said, in the back of your mind must always be the primary questions "What is my purpose?" and "What is the purpose of my job?"

First of all, your job provides money. It's what you do to facilitate success in all aspects of your life. The money provides for your family and for the more important things in your life. There will be times when you will need to create an imbalance in your life. If you are married and have a new baby, that baby will require considerable attention and care—other parts of your life will be secondary.

In the same way, there will be times when your job is your baby. If you are starting your own business, then the start-up will absolutely require more of your attention and effort. I have personally started four businesses from scratch—from the floor plans to the procedures to the promotions. I had to make many sacrifices. All four are successful to this day. It is true in all types of work, other parts of your life may have to receive less attention than they deserve. To a successful person, though, that imbalance will be temporary. Although an occasional imbalance is necessary for the entrepreneur who wants to succeed or the employee who has extra duties thrust upon him, if your job consumes all your attention and time, you need to recognize the imbalance and make adjustments.

What's difficult for high performers to realize is that job fulfillment is separate and different from self-fulfillment. A job should be rewarding and enjoyable. You should get a sense of accomplishment out of it. Ultimately, though, it is simply a part of your life that should be fulfilling as a whole. In other words, your work should be part of a fulfilling life. A fulfilling life is one in which you understand, pursue, and achieve your life's purpose.

However, your job is important in other ways. First of all, it reveals your character. If you are industrious, a hard worker, enjoy responsibility, and consider yourself conscientious, then those characteristics will show themselves in your work. Putting in eight or more hours a day will illustrate what you're made of.

The way you act at work will affect every other area of your life. Our true nature has a way of saturating every part of our lives no matter how we may try to compartmentalize it. If you are a high achiever at work and devote yourself to doing the very best job you can, that attitude will come through when you're helping your child with his homework, performing maintenance around the house, or trying to organize a bowling league. Make it a habit to give your all at work, and you will soon find the rewards showing up in all aspects of your life.

Performing the duties of your job is also part of the greater whole of your success journey. By now you understand that nothing in the universe is free. The job you do is part of the price you pay for your success. Giving your all in your job and career pays the price—going half-speed or giving less than your best effort is trying to get around paying the price. As we have discovered, the price for success will be paid. It's simply a matter of paying what you choose to pay or letting the universe decide for you.

The question of your job and your career is important because of one factor: you deserve to live the way you want to live. Whether you want financial security, a lavish lifestyle, or a simpler life, your choice of career will affect your ability to meet that desire.

There are sometimes questions about whether someone deserves what they have or not. The only criteria for worthiness is if you have paid the price for your life. People who always take the easy way out, make the easy choice, and avoid exerting any sort of effort will pay a price for their lifestyle. It may be in the form of chronic anxiety over finances or an inability to keep a job. For those who make the difficult choices, putting higher priorities over lesser ones, they are paying the price for the lifestyle they enjoy.

The law of reciprocation determines what we will enjoy in life. There may be temporary discouraging moments, but they are part of the process of achieving success in life. In the long run, giving your all at work will come back to reward you many times over.

What kind of life do you want to lead? That question seems easy to answer at first, but deeper thought on the matter may surprise you with its answer. We all lead dual lives. One is the life we are living, moment by moment, in the now. That's the part of us that is aware and uses our senses to get input from the world. We are always urged to stop and smell the roses along the way, and it's the you that is in the now that will enjoy the scent.

The other is the future you. Although we must live life now, we also prepare for the life we will lead tomorrow, the next day, and next year. It's the perfect image of this future you that keeps you focused on the success that you will enjoy. This perfect image is the graphic representation of the lifestyle that you choose. Your job and career choices are resources to help you realize that perfect image.

What kind of lifestyle do you choose for yourself? How do you choose to live? The answer to this must be based on the goals and priorities that you have set for yourself. For your life to be fulfilling, you must act in alignment with those goals and priorities.

How do you choose to "live" at work? For it to be such a major part of your life, you have to be able to conduct yourself in a way that corresponds with your values and priorities. You should be able to abide by your principles. As you conduct your business, take into consideration the values that you have chosen to live by. Are you acting the same way in your career as you want to act in the rest of your life? If you are having trouble reconciling your job with your principles, take some time to see what might need to be changed so that the two are in alignment.

Whether you work for yourself or for someone else, learn the habit of giving and receiving respect. In the urgency and deadlines of business, we sometimes forget to treat others the way we want to be treated. Respecting others indicates that you acknowledge their worth and that your own sense of self-worth demands that same respect from others.

Learn to always strive for excellence regardless of the task or job that you're asked to perform.

Learn to always strive for excellence regardless of the task or job that you're asked to perform. Live for your larger goals. Few jobs are ever done perfectly every time, but if your aim is to be excellent, then no one can ask any more of you. Maintain that standard all the time, and your reputation will be assured. Even if the task is simple, maybe even something you consider beneath you, give it your all so you will be ready to excel at those assignments that are more rewarding.

Love and respect the people you work with. Even if individuals act in a way that make it difficult, choose to respect and value the humanity in all of us. When you show respect for other human beings, regardless of their actions, the quality of your interactions will improve. You will have let them know that they have value.

Do your best to keep your work life and your personal life separate. Obviously there will be times when the two will overlap, such as company-sponsored family outings or when you invite someone from work to your home. What I mean here is that your job can be stressful, and it can harm your family life if you bring that stress home with you. Likewise, don't bring personal problems into your workplace. It won't help the personal issue, and it can only negatively affect your work.

You may have had discussions with someone at work about attitude. Performance reviews often have a category marked attitude. Exactly what is this concept that we hear so often but understand so little?

Bob Proctor says that your attitude is the combination of your thoughts, emotions, and actions. Positive or negative thoughts enter your mind; there they affect your emotions and prompt particular actions on your part. Because your actions are the only parts visible to everyone else, that's what they judge you on.

The truth is you directly control your attitude. Awareness and control of your attitude can have a profound impact on the rest of your life. First of all, take control of your mind. Decide which thoughts you will allow into your brain. You do this by choosing which people to associate with, to listen to, or to give credence to. Positive people lead to positive thoughts; negative people lead to negative thoughts.

Next, decide how much you will let thoughts affect your emotions. Many times we hear negative things and immediately our bodies respond, influencing our emotions. Be aware of the effect particular thoughts have on you. If you know in advance that discussing a certain topic affects you negatively, either avoid thinking about it or recognize when that particular button is pushed. We are, after all, human beings not machines. We have choices that we make, and one of the most important is how much we will let outside influences control us.

Follow the same process when you feel your emotions getting out of control. Although no one wants to be an emotionless android, it's not conducive to success to let your emotions lead you into actions that are destructive. Because your actions are the only part of your attitude visible to others, it's important that you control your actions. People judge you on what they see or hear you do.

The different elements of the entire process are what constitute your attitude. One thing about your attitude is that it is either a spiral up or a spiral down. A positive attitude now leads to a positive attitude later, and a negative attitude now leads to a negative attitude. Attitude becomes habit.

Exactly what is a positive attitude? Although sometimes we can't put it into words, most of us recognize a positive attitude when we see it. Generally a person with a positive attitude is smiling and upbeat. There is an aura of success and accomplishment around them. All the activity around them seems to be harmonious.

For someone who aspires to be a winner, a positive attitude leads to doing more than just enough. The winner does their share and checks to see if there's more that can be accomplished. It's been said that the enemy of great is "good enough." If the opportunity presents itself, the winner aims for the great.

Maintaining a positive attitude does not mean that you leave your brains at home when you go to work. Problems, bad situations, and challenges are all part of any workplace or project. Don't turn a blind eye to such things. On the contrary, with a positive attitude, you recognize such challenges and either solve them or refuse to let them affect your work.

At such a time, the winner evaluates his goals to make sure that what he is doing matches the bigger goals of the company as well as his own. He looks at the duties he is required to perform and the effects of his efforts. If they are all in line with his purpose, his values, and his goals, the winner shrugs and acknowledges that the situation is part of the price that he is willing to pay to be successful.

Your choice of attitude is important. Because the one aspect of any situation that you can control is how you react; your responses to challenges at work affect how you respond to challenges throughout the rest of your life. Conquering small challenges successfully gives you the strength and skill you need to beat larger challenges.

It's like a boxer who works out in the gym—jumping rope and punching the bag but never sparring with an opponent. The first time the boxer is in a bout with someone who is hitting back, he's unprepared. He has not tested himself to learn how to handle adversity.

Building your AQ (adversity quotient), or how much adversity you can take before you break, is critical to your current and future success. I recall learning this from Donald Trump.

How much can you handle before you give up, cry, or ask for help? What does it take to throw you off? Do you want a pilot or doctor with a high or low AQ? Look at the men and women who have forged and tempered a high AQ. They are the ones at the highest levels of success in every field.

When you have the ability to maintain a positive attitude through difficult circumstances at work, you are on your way to becoming a true success. That ability will translate into other situations that will require you to respond properly. Your value to your company will increase as you handle such situations.

When you have a positive attitude, your work environment will improve. You'll enjoy your work more if you associate positive feelings with it. By eliminating negative emotions from work, you condition yourself to expect enjoyment anytime you are working.

By making work more enjoyable you will also increase your productivity. When you get rid of negative distractions, your tasks become easier, and you accomplish more work. A harmonious atmosphere makes for better communication, which, in turn, leads to greater productivity.

Attitude is infectious. When one person has a positive attitude, everyone else around them is more inclined to share that attitude. The effect sometimes takes time, but the results are almost miraculous. All of the benefits of the positive atmosphere begin to take hold—better morale and more productivity, which benefits the company all around.

A positive attitude also marks you as a leader. Watch any group of people, and you will notice that the ones with a negative attitude form a clique. They don't want to hear anything positive. Everyone else will be drawn to the person with the positive attitude. People turn to them for advice and help. Eventually, the positive person will be known as a leader, the go-to guy who can get things done.

What should you expect from your job? Are achievement and recognition guaranteed? Although it would be nice to say that you will always be officially recognized for superior work, the truth is that it doesn't always happen. Setting your expectations to depend on other people to affirm your worth is a recipe for disappointment.

However, recognition is different from achievement. On every job, in every line of work, you should expect to have the opportunity to achieve. This is an expectation based on reality. As I mentioned earlier, you can excel in any position or task that you have. That pursuit of excellence is what will give you a sense of achievement. You will not have to depend on someone else for that pride of accomplishment.

The danger is in letting others affect your attitude in a negative way. You have to guard yourself against such influences. The negative thinkers may try to convince you that achievement is impossible, and there is no opportunity to excel. That's ridiculous, of course. But the chorus of jeers from such people can worm its way into your mind if you're not aware of the dangers.

What is achievement? It's taking the right actions to perform your duties and tasks at the highest level possible. It's going above and beyond what's expected of you so you are living up to your own expectations and not those of other people. When addressing a group at one of my coaching sessions, I have occasionally said, "When push comes to shove, who picks up the slack?" "We pick up the slack." Yes, that means you and I. Be the person who everyone knows will pick up the slack when needed. It may not be immediate, but you will always be rewarded.

You become an achiever when you look for opportunities to excel. You become a problem-solver—someone who presents solutions instead of complaining about the obstacles. You take the load off others around you, whether it's your boss, your co-workers, or customers. You try to lessen the burden of anyone who has an interest in the outcome of your task.

The key is to consider the big picture. Tunnel vision is always a threat; when you become so focused on your own small portion of the world, you forget what the bigger mission is. Having an outlook that encompasses the larger view opens your mind to new solutions and creative ways to solve problems.

Recognition differs from achievement in that you have to count on other people to provide recognition. While you can't count on or expect recognition for your achievements, it's nice to receive public acknowledgement of your efforts. Recognition is also good because it prepares the groundwork to move ahead in your career.

How do you go about getting recognized for your efforts? First of all, you have to perform. After that's done, though, don't hide your achievements. The Bible says, "Neither do men light a candle, and put it under a bushel, but on a candlestick; and it giveth light unto all that are in the house." Your achievement and recognition can inspire others to strive for excellence as well. Although you don't want to become known as a braggart, don't keep your efforts secret.

If you work for someone else, keep in mind that promotions come to those who receive recognition. When the decision-makers want to know who to promote, they look for those who can do the best job, and being recognized for your achievements puts you front and center in that search.

Remember to communicate your goals with the proper people. If you want a particular position, let your manager or supervisor know about your desire to move up. You must have the qualifications, of course, but making your interest known for a position is important. The decision-makers need to know of your interest, and it's up to you to make sure they have that information.

You may have realized by now that the attitude for success comes from within. Whether working for yourself or working for someone else, you must end the day knowing that you've done the best job you are capable of. If you can honestly say that you have given it your all, you can declare yourself successful. You define success for yourself—no one else can do it for you.

Evaluate your job and career to make sure it matches the larger purpose you have established for yourself. If you have chosen your career carefully and paid attention to your values and life purpose, then take advantage of the opportunity you have to create your successful career.

Use the Orange Card to fulfill your job and career goals. As always, define your purpose and make the image solid in your mind. If you have stayed true to your purpose and to the stakeholders involved, you will be truly successful in every sense of the word.

Points to Remember

You are not your job nor are you defined by it.

Your job is primarily one thing—it's what you do for money.

*For many people, the choice of job is one of the least
thought-out decisions they ever make.*

*To be good at your job, you must provide
value to all stakeholders.*

Job fulfillment is separate and different from self-fulfillment.

Your job is important in that it reveals character.

*Performing your job duties is part of the greater
whole of your success journey.*

The law of reciprocation determines what we will enjoy in life.

*Whether you work for yourself or for someone else, learn the
habit of giving and receiving respect.*

*Your attitude is the combination of your
thoughts, emotions, and actions.*

Your attitude is directly under your control.

*On every job, in every line of work, you should expect
to have the opportunity to achieve.*

When it comes to work, Quality + Quantity = Compensation!

The attitude for success comes from within.

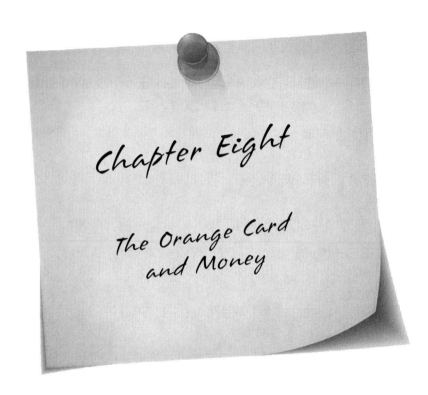

Chapter Eight

The Orange Card
and Money

– THE ORANGE CARD AND MONEY –

"He that is of the opinion money will do everything may well be suspected of doing everything for money."

— Benjamin Franklin

How do I become a millionaire?

What is compound interest, and why is it important?

Can compound interest work against me?

What are some of the misconceptions about money?

How do millionaires get their money?

A ccording to *"The Wealth Report"* (WSJ.com), there were 8.3 million millionaires in the United States in 2006. Additionally, there were 371 billionaires. For anyone who aspires to increase their wealth, those numbers are inspiring. Not only is becoming wealthy possible, it's not even unusual.

Since the dawn of civilization, there have been wealthy people. In every society, in every culture, in every type of economy, there have been opportunities for individuals to work and create their own wealth. When the weather is hot and dry, the lemonade stand is busy. If it rains, the umbrella salesman gets rich. If there is one rule that is constant, it is that conditions will always change. And in any new situation, there will be opportunities for people with vision, courage, and the willingness to work to become wealthy.

When it comes to becoming wealthy, there are no new rules and no surprises. Even with technological advancement creating new opportunities and new avenues of advertising, marketing, and distribution, the old rules still apply. People become millionaires using basic principles.

That's why anyone can become an "automatic" millionaire. It's a simple matter of mathematics, and numbers don't change based on who you are. Numbers and equations are constant and can be counted on for everything from constructing a bridge to launching a space shuttle to becoming a millionaire.

For example, compound interest is a concept that millionaires take advantage of. Basically, compound interest is when interest—extra money earned on another sum of money (called principle)—is earned on interest. For example, if you have $100 in a savings account and earn 10 percent interest annually (called the annual percentage rate or APR), at the end of the first year you'll have $110. The next year, you will earn interest on $110 (the principle plus the interest you earned the first year), and at the end of the year you will have $121. That's compound interest.

Rich people get that way by understanding compound interest. They put their money into accounts or funds that earn money and watch the money grow through the power of compound interest. A nice rule to know is the rule of seventy-two: divide the interest rate you're earning into seventy-two, and that tells you how long it will take for your money to double. For example, if you earn 6 percent on your savings account, divide seventy-two by six and the answer is twelve. Your money will double in twelve years.

Unfortunately, the average American learns about compound interest the hard way, and their instructors are the credit card companies. The average credit card holder will carry a balance over from one month to the next. Interest is applied to the balance, and that becomes the balance due the next month. The card holder will once again carry over a balance, and interest is applied to that balance, which includes the interest applied the month before.

Credit card companies take advantage of the power of compound interest by encouraging their customers to pay a minimum payment, thereby ensuring that a balance will be carried over. By paying the minimum payment on a two-thousand dollar initial charge, you would make payments on that card for nearly thirty years, even if you never charged another thing. Congress has recently enacted legislation to force credit card companies to double their minimum payments—ostensibly to give consumers the chance to pay off their debts quicker.

So on the one hand, rich people get rich by earning compound interest, and average people pay compound interest. The math is the same in both instances. The only difference is how people apply it.

That's why becoming a millionaire can be automatic. By applying basic principles—use compound interest, pay yourself first, and live below your means, for example—that have been proven time and time again by others, anyone has the means to become wealthy. The only thing holding most people back is their own mindset.

The concept of becoming wealthy may be a new concept to you. Many people have been indoctrinated to the point where they ask, "Why is money so important?" The simple answer is that even if money is unimportant to you, you can bet that it's important to your electric company, your grocer, your gas station, and your credit card company.

Even if you believe that money is unimportant, you have to face the fact that our lives are built around the principles of using money to acquire those goods and services that we require to live. Even if you long for a simpler time when everything was based on trade and barter, you have to ask yourself, "If that system was so good, why was money ever created?" The answer, of course, is that money is necessary for any lifestyle above a subsistence existence.

Today the need for money is more complex, but no less important. In a country that has the resources available to create over eight million millionaires, a shocking number of people live in poverty. Many retirees, through poor or inadequate planning, spend their later years living well below the standard they enjoyed while they were employed. Try asking any of those people if money is important.

Money has one key attribute. When you have money, you are independent instead of dependent. With enough money, you can make decisions based on how you will improve your life rather than if you can afford it or not. A friend has an emergency fund that he calls his "get lost" money. He has enough put away so that if his employer ever tries to force him to do something that is against his values or that he doesn't want to do, he can simply quit and live quite comfortably. To people like this, money has become less important rather than more. He has acquired the ability to make his decisions based on higher-level principles.

It's safe to say that people who have lived and planned their lives in such a way will not be a burden to others. Too many people count on others— their family, the government, or charities—for their needs. Some of these people obviously have physical or mental impairments that make caring for themselves impossible. But many more are in their positions because of decisions they made throughout their lives.

Even for those who are getting by, maintaining a lifestyle can be difficult and time-consuming. Americans live in the land of the free and the home of the broke. We are surrounded by a society in which indulging the appetite is the primary concern, regardless of the cost. Advertisers show the latest shiny gadget or toy, and we become eager to do whatever it takes to have it. That includes going into debt—often so deeply that there seems to be no way out.

I maintain that quality of life is not measured by how much stuff you have but by how much you enjoy the stuff you have. And it's impossible to fully enjoy your stuff if you're constantly worried about making the payments on it.

"All right," I can hear you say, "I can do a lot better with my money—but a millionaire? That's crazy."

What's crazy is ignoring the fact that almost everyone who is active in the workplace will have a million dollars. If you figure that the average person begins his adult work life at age twenty-two and retires at age sixty-five—that's a work life of forty-three years. They would earn a million dollars by averaging an annual wage of a little more than $23,000.

Most people will earn well over a million dollars in their lifetimes. The problem is not earning a million dollars but keeping it because in addition to earning a million dollars in our lifetime, we'll also spend a million dollars. Where does it all go?

If you smoke a pack of cigarettes a day from age twenty to age sixty-five, and if a pack of cigarettes costs $5, you'll spend $82,125 on cigarettes in your lifetime.

If you drink a single soft drink each day for the same period of time, you'll spend over $16,000 for your habit.

If you dine out once a week, averaging $50 for a meal, you'll spend $117,000 eating in restaurants.

That's already nearly a quarter of a million dollars, and we haven't even mentioned buying a house ($246,100 median price in 2007) or your car (a new or used car every three years with an average price of $20,000, you'll spend about $300,000 on cars in your lifetime; plus maintenance, repairs, insurance, taxes, and financing).

If you'll earn a fortune in your lifetime, then clearly the key to becoming wealthy is how you handle the money you already have. How did all of these millionaires get to be that way? Did they inherit it? Win the lottery?

Some did, of course, but fewer than you might think. In their amazing book *The Millionaire Next Door,* Thomas Stanley and William Danko researched America's rich to find out how they got that way. They discovered that 80 percent of millionaires did not inherit their wealth. In other words, most of American millionaires are first-generation rich. Here are a few of their other findings:

- Two-thirds of those still working are self-employed.

- Ninety-seven percent are homeowners with about half of those having lived in the same home for twenty years or more.

- Eighty percent have college degrees.

- They save at least 15 percent of their income.

- Only 19 percent received any money from a trust fund or estate. More than half never received a dollar from an inheritance.

Additionally, the millionaires studied lived well below their means. They drove less expensive cars, wore less expensive clothing, and, generally, were more frugal with their money than the typical American.

Besides budgeting their money tightly and being aware of where their money went, the millionaires believed "charity begins at home," and they paid themselves first. Clearly something is going on in the minds of these millionaires that other people haven't grasped or else we'd all be millionaires. What could possibly be the difference?

One factor is the beliefs that we hold about money. The English language is sprinkled with various sayings about money—"you can't take it with you," "money isn't everything," and "money is made to be spent"—that reflect the negative views many people have about money.

Two sayings stand out in how often they are quoted by people with negative attitudes about money, usually with a triumphant smirk at having won the argument. The first is "Money is the root of all evil." This is a partial quote from 1 Timothy 6:10. The full quote is very revealing: "For the love of money is the root of all sorts of evil." Although there is no doubt that money is important, such things as our relationships with our family and our relationship with a higher power are much more valuable. The phrase was probably intentionally misquoted originally as someone tried to make a point, which changed the meaning of the original saying.

Another commonly used Bible verse is Matthew 19:24: "It is easier for a camel to go through the eye of a needle than for a rich man to enter the kingdom of God." This quote from Jesus is used to try to prove that rich people are evil. What's missing is the context.

The story is about a rich man who asks Jesus how to get to heaven. When told to divest himself of all his worldly goods, the man refuses and walks away. The point of the story is, once again, that some things are more important than money. Jesus knew the man was unable to let go of his worldly possessions and said the quote to illustrate the point. The verse is not about any moral judgment on money or those who have it—only about those who value money above all else. Money isn't, and shouldn't be, everything.

It's clear that many people hold very negative beliefs about money. They will go to great lengths to defend the fact that they don't have any. Rather than admit that they have made choices which prevented them from accumulating wealth, they try to convince other people they have made the moral decision not to have money.

People with such a view have a poverty mentality. They feel that if one person wins, then someone else has to lose. If one person earns a dollar, then someone else had to lose a dollar. The entire universe is a zero-sum game.

The reality is, of course, much different. As far as the universe is concerned, there is no difference between earning one dollar or earning a million dollars. In other words, there is an abundance of riches available for anyone who is willing to work hard and make the decisions that are required to become wealthy. Those who protest other people's wealth have simply not done that.

An abundance mentality is necessary to become rich. You have to understand the fact that there is enough for everyone. The fact that escapes most people is that you have to add value to life in order to increase your own wealth. By adding value, you are increasing the wealth that is available to other people as well as yourself. Like those millionaires mentioned above who are self-employed or own their own businesses, wealth is earned by giving to the world around you. This is the belief that most people miss.

Why don't they have that belief? The same reasons that people hold incorrect and nonproductive beliefs about anything—poor programming. Most of us learn about money and wealth (or lack of it) from our parents. Whereas most people are not rich because of poor decision-making, most learned the wrong lessons. We had bad role models.

The good news is you can still achieve the kind of wealth you deserve. Just like the 80 percent of millionaires who are first-generation rich, you can overcome your programming and succeed at a level that most people only dream of. Because while they are satisfied with dreaming, you are ready to take action to get what you want.

What are some of the more common wealth-destroying beliefs? One common belief is that somehow money, debt, and bills will work themselves out. This is literally a lottery mentality where, regardless of the kind of decisions you make, something will come through for you and make everything all right.

Nothing could be further from the truth, of course. The millionaires studied knew exactly where their money was going. They budgeted their income and expenses and planned their savings, investments, and retirement. They lived below their means, often with a lower-level lifestyle than their considerably less-rich neighbors. They looked for bargains and didn't knowingly waste a penny.

Again, this is one of those automatic principles that can make you wealthy. Be aware of your money and where it goes, and get the most out of every dollar. That means you pay less in interest, penalties, fees, and taxes. You deny impulses that can destroy your wealth-building plan and focus on maximizing every dollar.

Wealthy people accumulate assets that will increase in value. Poor people accumulate items that are either consumed or which rapidly lose their value. To become wealthy, you want to emulate what rich people do. It's as simple as consciously deciding how you're going to spend your money. Money never works itself out—it must be controlled.

Another common belief is that money is bad or immoral. Again, this philosophy is expressed by people who have made decisions that led to not having any money. Clearly, pieces of paper and metal coins have no morality. Money only represents purchasing power, so there is no moral or immoral factor there.

In fact, what they really mean is that people who have money are bad or immoral. There is a basis of truth to the statement—rich people are human beings and as such are guilty of some of the same behaviors as poor and middle-class people. Within any group of people, there will be some who are good and some who are bad and some who are moral and some who are immoral.

My point is that questionable behavior is not restricted to any type or class. Having money or not having money does not determine if you're a good person or not. It might even be argued that if a person is willing to work hard, add value to the world, control his impulses, and live within his means so as not to be a burden to others, he is well on his way to becoming a good person. Is it a coincidence that those are the same characteristics that will help you become wealthy?

Another example of a poor outlook toward money is fatalism and personalizing incidents. That's the type of mentality that says, "If I invest in this stock, it's sure to go down." A variation on this is, "If I root for this team, they're sure to lose." I'm sure you've heard similar statements.

A simple way to defuse this mentality is to realize this: The stock doesn't know you own it. The idea behind this outlook is fear—fear that is fed by the false programming and mistaken beliefs of others who don't know how to achieve their dreams. It's a fact of life that those who have lived a subpar life are always afraid of someone else achieving their heart's desire. Accepting a false outlook is becoming infected by another person's fears. If you want an adage to remember, try this one: fortune favors the bold.

Financial guru Dave Ramsey has a saying: "Achieving your financial goals is 20 percent knowledge and 80 percent behavior." The exact percentages are not important. What is important is embracing the idea that the way you act controls more of your success with money than having extensive knowledge. More important than either of these, however, is that your beliefs are right. Rich people first had certain beliefs that made them rich, and the knowledge and actions followed those beliefs.

One wealth-minded belief is that the primary thing money can buy you is freedom. Remember the "get lost" fund mentioned earlier? A person with that kind of attitude and wealth can walk away from any situation or job. They are no longer bound by the worry of "what will I do?" They have the luxury of being able to live to the highest principles they hold, making decisions based on their value system rather than concern over their finances.

Another belief that rich people hold is that they must offer something of value in order to be paid for it. Many of the millionaires in Stanley and Danko's book *The Millionaire Next Door,* were business owners, and most of them owned unglamorous, mundane, normal companies. They were drycleaners, pest control service operators, and diesel engine repairers. The millionaires were able to provide a service or a product that people valued and would pay for.

After all, money is simply a medium that is exchanged for something of value.

After all, money is simply a medium that is exchanged for something of value. If you offer something of enough value, people will pay any price for it. The value of the product or service can only be determined by the person who pays for it. Many baseball fans become irate at the multi-million dollar contracts that major league players receive and cry, "Nobody's worth that much." The truth is, the value of the player is determined by the team paying the salary. To the person who places enough value on a player to pay millions of dollars, he is indeed worth it.

The simple concept for anyone aspiring to become wealthy is this: Offer a service or product of great value to the world. The greater the value you offer, the more money you will receive.

A *Forbes* magazine article cited studies of lottery winners, which revealed that after winning, many of the winners suffer broken relationships and become estranged from their families and friends. Those who have received sudden wealth have spoken about the isolation they feel as they deal with the emotional challenges stemming from the shift in their circumstances. Thayer Willis, author of the book *Navigating the Dark Side of Wealth,* puts it best: "People who are dealing with these challenges of wealth know that most people won't sympathize… Their attitude is 'I should have your problems.'"

When your riches come to you—as they will—you'll need to make sure you are paying attention to the relationships in your life. Questions will arise about different aspects of relationships, and the health of your associations may be in danger. Anticipate these changes and address them as you work toward creating your wealth. When those around you understand that you care about them, they will be more open to accepting the new you that you are creating.

Some specific questions arise that are consistent any time someone begins to do well financially. For example, should you lend money to a friend or a relative? Being a lender changes the dynamic of the relationship. If a friend or relative is in debt to you, despite your best efforts, there will be tension, especially if the friend or relative gets behind on payments. It's been said that Thanksgiving dinner tastes different when you owe money to the person across the table.

What's the answer? You have several options, of course. You could simply say no and leave it at that. If you have been consistent in declining requests for loans before, then your answer won't be unexpected. If, on the other hand, you were free with lending your money before, a sudden change in attitude will fuel the resentment they might feel at being declined.

Another solution is to give the money as a gift. If the person is genuinely in need and you are in a position to help, you can avoid some of the pitfalls of being a lender to those close to you. If they protest, tell them that the payback is to help someone else who is in need when the opportunity arises.

Business ventures seem to pop up whenever you attain wealth. Beyond a loan, investing in a business can obligate you to ongoing losses and possibly liability. Those close to you may try to trade on the relationship to get you to invest in a "great opportunity." If you feel someone is trying to make you feel guilty in order to get you to invest in a questionable venture, call it to his attention immediately. Say something like, "I'm beginning to feel a little pressured to do this. I'm sure that's not what you are trying to do."

As you attain more wealth, start researching professionals who can help you deal with these situations. Refer any requests for business investments to your financial advisor. He will be able to evaluate the risks and rewards in a nonemotional manner and make appropriate recommendations.

This section has not been intended to create paranoia. Instead, I want to remind you that there are possible pitfalls ahead that, with caution and preparation, can be avoided. As you increase your wealth, spend time working on your relationships so they are strong enough to survive your success. Part of the enjoyment of being rich is having someone to share the fun with.

A major factor that prevents people from becoming rich is their addiction to debt. According to the Consumer Federation of America, Americans carry almost $900 million in debt on their credit cards alone. Add that to the auto loans, home mortgages, school loans, and personal loans, and you have the picture of a society that has made debt part of its fabric.

Debt is an anchor that will weigh you down just as you are trying to take flight. Remember one of the things wealth buys you is freedom. If you have debt, then your freedom is curtailed to the extent that you're in debt. Becoming debt free will make the path to realizing your wealth that much easier.

After graduating from professional school, I had over $128,000 in student loan debt. After paying $1,000 per month for eight years—$96,000—I still owed $122,000! I was so furious by how the interest was so front loaded that I dug in and focused my efforts.

I had the student loans paid by the end of the next year. I gave the student loan company a "get lost" of my own. You can too! In the financial fitness area of my consulting, I am very willing to show people how to truly deal with debt and start saving real money for the future because I have done it myself.

The millionaires mentioned earlier believed in living below their means and carrying no debt. They have extra money because they have chosen to control their appetites, and they have established increasing their wealth as a priority. They understand how using their money to earn interest is a better way to become (and stay) rich than paying interest.

We discussed how achieving millionaire status is not complex. The formula has been established, and following that formula is the surest way to increase your own fortune. It may go against all your own programming to eliminate debt, but the experience of the millionaires has made it clear that the attitude of living without debt will make the goal that much easier to reach.

When you establish your priorities and determine your purpose regarding attaining wealth, you will outline the best course for you personally to achieve your goal. If you carry debt, you are working against your own efforts.

So you've determined that you are going to get out of debt so you can reach your wealth goals easier and quicker. How do you go about getting out of debt?

The first step is to stop adding more debt! Debt is like a hole in a leaky lifeboat—you can bail water like crazy, but if you're making the hole bigger as you go, you're wasting time and energy. Why make your task more difficult?

Our culture will try to work against you in this endeavor. Everyone receives credit card offers in the mail—people have even reported their pets getting offers! America is a consumption-oriented society, and the companies that profit from your debt are experts at marketing that debt to you.

Establish your priorities according to your values, and you will be able to resist these distractions. Every time you see an offer for something new, think to yourself, "They're trying to keep me from being rich, and I won't let them!"

A sad fact is that many people are current with their credit card companies but behind on their home mortgages, rent, or even groceries. They have forgotten how to establish and follow their priorities. In grade school, we all learned the three basic needs that humans have—food, clothing, and shelter. These are the important, urgent items that people should pay for before paying consumer debt like credit cards, furniture, or even cars.

The reason is that debt collectors have become expert at using the best psychological tricks available to squeeze money out of people who are too timid to resist. Collectors will use shame, guilt, and intimidation to force consumers to pay the credit card before they pay their house payment.

You are not one of these people (at least not anymore). Using the Orange Card technique, you have established your purpose and are working in the most efficient way possible to accumulate wealth. Other people have shown you the way, and all you have to do is follow their example. It's automatic.

If you have trouble working on your debt, attack it in small increments. Create a written budget to control your spending and to make sure you're taking care of your priorities first. Establish an emergency fund so that unexpected situations don't throw you completely out of your game plan.

Who do millionaires pay first? Themselves! They will take a certain amount or percentage out of each paycheck and put it into savings or investments. When you take care of the important items first, then the unimportant distractions that follow can't do as much damage to you. And paying yourself first is the key. Regardless of what happens afterward, the wealth-building portion has been allotted. No distractions or minor emergencies can throw you off when you've taken care of your top priority.

In order to become a winner, you first have to define winning. Sure, becoming wealthy is great, but that's merely the end result. What is the mindset that separates the rich from the not rich?

First you have to think of yourself as a builder not a consumer. You are constructing your own private castle, built on the principles most important to you. That castle will represent your adhering to what's most important in your life and your discarding of those items and habits that prevent others from achieving their dreams.

Another belief that you need to keep in mind is that, although you work hard and attaining wealth is important to you, money does not control you. Guided by your values and principles, you are able to resist the temptation to take shortcuts simply to make money. Remember the universal law that says there will always be a price to pay for success. You can control yourself and name your own price, or you can try to get around the law—in which case the price you pay will not be of your own choosing and will be infinitely greater than you expect.

As a wealth-minded individual, you resolve not to worry about money. Worry is simply becoming anxious about something that has not occurred and over which you have no control. By following the same path that other millionaires before you have followed, you have taken the steps over which you have some measure control. Worrying about money lessens the enjoyment of having it. Be aware, be prudent, be smart, and you will have no need to worry about money ever again.

The ultimate goal of being rich is to live the kind of life you want to live. Your path to wealth will likely involve some self-sacrifice, and you want to make sure you control your appetites and not let them control you. However, you have the right to enjoy the life that you build for yourself and your family. If you have paid the price beforehand, there is no point in denying yourself any of the necessities.

Money, and the things that it buys, are supposed to be enjoyed. To access the full pleasure available to you from attaining wealth, take care of the important items first—then relax. Your labors deserve to be rewarded so that you will be motivated to continue to do the things that made you successful in the first place.

Throughout this section, I have emphasized the word control. Control your appetites, debt, spending, and budget. Stanley and Danko call this playing defense. Regardless of your income, playing defense must be part of your strategy if you want to achieve wealth.

The other side of the equation is playing offense—earning money. Most of the millionaires in Stanley and Danko's book had high incomes. As either business owners and/or highly-paid professionals, they used their skills to increase their incomes dramatically. To win at money, you must be proficient at both offense and defense.

There are basically three types of income: active, passive, and portfolio. Active income is the money that you earn directly from your participation. People maximize their active income by getting college degrees and/or learning a skill in a field that pays well. This is where planning and discipline are vital.

Too many people fall into their careers through apathy. They may take a job that is completely uninvolved with what they went to school for. Through their inaction, they wind up on a career path that leads to a lower income than they are capable of earning elsewhere. It takes research and effort to find the right job in the right place at the right pay. If you want to increase your income, then you have to prepare yourself so that you are qualified and in place for the job that will pay you the most.

Passive income is money you earn without active participation. Dividends and royalties are examples of passive income. Royalties are a special case because they provide income on work that was done previously. Although they result from your past active participation, they're included in this category because the new income results from other people using your intellectual property without additional participation on your part.

Rich people derive a large part of their wealth through passive income. Passive income provides leverage that helps them get the maximum income for their efforts. Although the income is described as passive, most millionaires are decidedly active in their analysis, homework, and attention that goes into choosing which investments they want to put their money into.

You earn portfolio income through buying and selling for a profit. Stocks and real estate are examples of portfolio income. It's important that we don't confuse assets with income. Although millionaires often possess millions of dollars in assets, these are not considered income unless and until they sell the assets. Millionaires increase their net worth by investing in and holding onto assets that appreciate in value.

Although lottery winners are often millionaires—at least for a while—lottery winnings is not a useful category. The majority of millionaires realize that it's through their own efforts that they will become wealthy. They don't waste money unnecessarily but put their money into projects where the odds are in their favor.

Remember that there are three categories of wealth. The first is those with income wealth. These are people who have decent incomes that are being completely spent on lots of monthly payments, thus giving them the trappings of wealth. Those people want to look rich.

There are also those who play the "net worth game," running around talking about how much all their stuff is supposedly worth, thus making themselves feel rich.

Then there is the third category, and the one we all truly want to be in—cash wealth. These are people like you and I who have saved and accumulated real money. Those are the ones who know how to be rich. You can choose the one you like.

The Orange Card system is the tool that will help you become wealthy. Use the card to focus your energies and efforts, and the path to wealth is clear. Picture yourself as a wealthy person living the life you want. You are enjoying the lifestyle your hard work has earned you. You have paid the price the universal laws demand you pay. Success in attaining riches and living a rich lifestyle is within your grasp as long as you understand and apply the principles underlying the process.

The riches are already within you. Your application of the universal laws will help you manifest those spiritual riches into physical wealth.

Profile: Donald Trump

DONALD TRUMP OWNS SOME of the most high-profile properties in New York City. Through good fortune and bad, Trump has managed to keep his status as a celebrity as well as his reputation as the prime real estate developer in New York City.

Donald Trump was one of five children of Fred Trump, a property developer. Donald was high-spirited as a boy, and his parents sent him to military school in an attempt to help him learn discipline. He thrived in that environment, and eventually he attended the Wharton School of Business.

After graduating from college, Trump worked for his father for five years and learned the details of the real estate development business. His father was a huge influence, and Trump has acknowledged that influence, saying, "My father was my mentor, and I learned a tremendous amount about every aspect of the construction industry from him."

The elder Trump was impressed with his son's skills, remarking that everything he touches "seems to turn to gold." Donald was ambitious, however, and had larger visions than his father. He successfully renovated the Commodore Hotel in New York City, and it became the Grand Hyatt—an instant success that put Trump's name on the real estate development map.

In the ensuing years, Donald Trump has built a real estate empire that has garnered him millions of dollars, as well as fame. An extravagant and self-confident businessman, Trump has managed to parlay his business success into notoriety as a celebrity and lead a high-profile life that keeps his name in the news.

Trump also demonstrates the benefit of being a giver as well as accumulating wealth. He is well known as a philanthropist, giving millions of dollars to various charities and lending his name to others to help raise funds. Trump clearly understands that his fortunes can help others as well as himself, and despite his public reputation as hard-nosed and businesslike, his interest in helping charities shows a balance that might escape casual inspection.

Trump has also expanded his interests beyond real estate. He has authored several books on business, introduced an innovative online business school, and hosts a popular television program. His success as a businessman is the most well-known aspect of Donald Trump's life, but he truly understands the need for balance and the need to expand beyond his comfort zone in his own pursuit of success.

Points to Remember

Becoming wealthy is not only possible, it's not even unusual.

In every economic condition there have been opportunities for individuals to work hard and create their own wealth.

People become millionaires by applying basic principles.

Rich people take advantage of compound interest while poor people are taken advantage of by compound interest.

Money has one key attribute—when you have money, you are independent instead of dependent.

Most Americans live in the land of the free and the home of the broke.

The challenge is not in earning a million dollars, it's keeping it.

Holding negative attitudes about money is the reason most people are not wealthy.

*There is an abundance of riches available for
anyone who is willing to work hard and make
the decisions required to become wealthy.*

*By adding value, you are increasing the wealth that is
available to other people as well as yourself.*

*Be aware of your money, where it goes,
and get the most out of every dollar.*

*Wealthy people accumulate assets that will increase
in value. Poor people accumulate items that are either
consumed or that rapidly lose their value.*

*Fatalism and fear are fed by the false programming
and mistaken beliefs of others who don't know
how to achieve their dreams.*

The primary thing money can buy you is freedom.

*A simple concept for anyone aspiring to become wealthy is
this: Offer a service or product of great value to the world. The
greater the value you offer, the more money you will receive.*

*When your riches come to you, pay special attention
to the relationships in your life.*

*Debt is an anchor that will weigh you down
just as you are trying to take flight.*

Millionaires pay themselves first.

*To accumulate wealth, think of yourself as
a builder not a consumer.*

*Although attaining wealth is important to you, money
does not control you. Remember—we love people and
use money, not the other way around.*

*The ultimate goal of being rich is to share and
live the kind of life you want to live.*

*There are basically three types of
income—active, passive, and portfolio.*

*The Orange Card system is the tool that will help you
become wealthy. Use the card to focus your energies
and efforts, and the path to wealth is clear.*

Chapter Nine

When You Lose Focus

−WHEN YOU LOSE FOCUS−

"A mind troubled by doubt cannot focus on the course to victory."

— Arthur Golden

I'm off track. What do I do?

What causes people to backslide?

How do I regain focus?

How do I handle fear?

How do I avoid setbacks in the future?

In Greek mythology, Sisyphus was punished by the gods for believing that he was as clever as they were. His punishment for all eternity was to roll a huge stone up a steep hill, only to have the stone roll back down before he could reach the top. The frustrating nature of the punishment was reserved for Sisyphus because he had the audacity to consider himself the equal of the gods.

We sometimes suffer the same type of frustration. We are enjoying success, everything is going according to plan, then all of a sudden, things go wrong, and we don't know why. We have pushed the stone up the hill only to have it roll down, leaving us shocked that it happened. With all the careful planning and consideration of our purpose and having paid the price, why isn't success automatic?

If you have suffered a setback like this, don't feel alone. Everyone who has tried to accomplish something worthwhile has had setbacks. For us, a setback is defined as any time when your progress toward your goal has stalled unexpectedly or even gone backward.

Even with a successful plan, we will occasionally anticipate a time when movement toward a goal appears to have stalled. Conditions may have to be adjusted, the particular step may require time to come to fruition, or some other cause may make it look, to an outsider, as though your progress has stopped.

Anticipated delays are not setbacks. They are a natural part of the universe. Setbacks are the times when you are caught off guard and don't know what happened. When Robert Burns wrote the lines "The best-laid plans of mice and men/go oft awry," he knew what he was talking about. Even with plenty of planning and preparation, your success plan may get thrown off by external factors.

What causes setbacks in a success plan? It can be a number of factors. Probably the most common is that you lose your sense of purpose. As we saw earlier, the Orange Card program emphasizes that you have to know your purpose in any endeavor before you can take the proper steps to become successful.

Losing sight of your purpose may be due to fatigue. Staying focused can be physically and mentally draining. If you have neglected yourself physically, you may simply need to take some down time in order to refresh yourself and recharge your batteries. When you're ready to concentrate on the steps to accomplish your purpose, then get busy and back on track.

Loss of focus is another success killer. Sometimes the phenomenal success you enjoy can cause you to lose focus. It works like this—every part of your plan is working so well that you decide to add just a little bit more to your plate. You may take on extra volunteer responsibilities, or you may decide to start a big project or something else equally ambitious.

Before you know it, you are covered up with tasks that have nothing to do with achieving your purpose. You have let yourself get caught up, and trivial matters—trivial at least in realizing your dreams—have taken over your life. They have pushed out the more important things you should be doing.

The solution to this is obvious. You have to eliminate anything that is distracting you from your goals. If you have been honest with yourself throughout the process, you have established your priorities based on your values and the larger purpose you have established for your life. You know the things you should be doing. Compare how you ought to spend your time against how you are actually spending it, and you'll quickly see what needs to go.

You may have been distracted from your purpose by a new factor in your life. It may be a new romance, a new car, or a new hobby. It can be any number of things. What these things have in common is the ability to take up your attention. If you find yourself spending more time on your hobby than on your success plan, then you may have let things get out of hand. Evaluate the time you spend on distractions to see if they have thrown you off course.

A big factor that can lead to a major setback is fear. Even if—sometimes especially if—you have enjoyed sudden success along the way, you may feel as though you are progressing faster than you can handle. Your fear stems from the old programming trying to exert its influence again.

Guilt from the past and fear about the future tend to shackle people's minds, rendering them ineffective in the present. This is one of my favorite topics to teach at seminars, and the solution is simple—forgiveness. Forgiveness eliminates guilt, and thankfulness washes out fear. This allows you to pay attention and do a better job in the moment.

Present-time consciousness is crucial to your success and happiness. Do this exercise: while driving down the road, say "Thank you" and "I forgive you" to every car you see passing by. Better yet, call or picture in your mind the people you need to forgive and say "I forgive you" over and over. Get it out. Few things will elevate your all-powerful self-image more than honest forgiveness on your part.

Remember that you have thought your plan through carefully and decided that your goals are worthwhile and apply to your purpose. You have determined that you are willing to pay the price for success. When irrational fear rears its ugly head, squash it with the confidence that you are doing the right thing, and if anyone ever deserved success, it's you.

Difficult though it might be, when this fear of success hits, try to remember that this is actually a good sign. It means that you are achieving the success that you have strived so hard to attain. Your bad programming is fighting to survive because it can't deal with the reality of your success. When this happens, it's time to kill the old programming once and for all.

Take a deep breath and tell yourself that you are going to achieve your success because you deserve it. You have done all the right things and the law of attraction will not be denied. Your old programming was set before you found something better—the Orange Card. The Orange Card works for you, and the old, incorrect programming doesn't.

Any time you feel fear because your success comes to you quickly, remember that achieving success was the plan all along. Kill the fear with the truth—you will be successful, and you won't be denied.

You know you're suffering a setback when you begin to have the feeling that you're sitting still. Remember that success involves movement—lose that movement and you are beginning to lose momentum.

You may also begin to lose excitement over achieving your goal. That excitement is what should motivate you. Any time you picture the image in your mind of living the successful life you want, you should feel a tingle up your spine.

If you are the type of person who enjoys numbers, then use them to see if you are moving forward or if you've stalled. Numbers don't lie—if your measurements don't match your projections, find out what's wrong and correct it.

Many setbacks can be avoided if you remain aware of where you are and what you're trying to achieve. That awareness is what makes wealthy people check on their investments periodically to see how they're doing. It's also what makes pilots run through their checklist before every flight. Awareness is one of the best attributes you can ever have.

As mentioned before, establishing milestones can help you prevent setbacks. Stay on top of your numbers, and you will find that things go much more smoothly. Use measurements—weight, time, dollars, or number of sales—to provide you with markers along the way, and you will instantly recognize if you are on schedule with your success plan.

Once you realize that you've gotten off track, how do you recover from a setback? First of all, you have to become a problem solver. Think through the issue to determine exactly when and where you went wrong. Did something occur about the same time you lost your sense of excitement? Did a bad month throw you behind, and you've never recovered?

Write down all the things related to the situation. Remember to write down the issues and notice how small they become. That is why this technique is sometimes called reducing your thoughts to writing, as the problem instantly becomes easier to fix once you get it down on paper.

After you've found the cause, figure out what you need to do to get back on your plan. Decide if you need to make a major change or if you can tinker with your process to make sure it's working like you want it to. The most important thing is to have the mindset that whatever it is, you're going to fix it.

You may discover that you are working the wrong plan. You shouldn't have this problem if you have been honest in your answers and faithful to the plan, but occasionally you will have priorities change, and now you need to change your plan.

Something this fundamental requires a wholesale reworking of your plan to encompass your priorities. Incorporate as much as you can of what you have done into the new plan so that you can start ahead of the game. Remember that the process is the same regardless of what your goals are. Only the details change.

As we mentioned earlier, sudden success catches some people by surprise and throws them off their game plan. Think about success for a moment and the changes it may bring to your life. You may have more money, better health, a better love life, and a better career—everything you wanted. What changes will this cause in your lifestyle?

One of the surest signs of success is when you start receiving criticism from those who have given up on life.

Whatever your goal is, prepare for success now. Anticipate it, and prepare for the changes that success will bring to your life. Just as you pack your luggage depending on your destination, you want to be ready for the new life that you are bringing about.

If you anticipate changes, you won't be caught off guard when they happen. Follow the Orange Card program, and you will achieve success. Be ready for it.

One of the surest signs of success is when you start receiving criticism from those who have given up on life. As you move forward, they see themselves being left further and further behind. They will do everything they can to pull you back. Don't let this happen. You've determined that you are going to be successful, and no one is going to stop you.

You'll hear variations on all the old programming that you've eliminated from your life. People who try to hold you back will push every button they can think of to stop you from reaching your goal. You'll recognize these people—they're bitter because they have given up. They'll try to hurt you with their remarks.

The people you want to keep close are those who encourage you to continue your ascent. These are the people who understand what you're trying to accomplish, and they will help you along the way. Positive people produce positive results, so surround yourself with those people.

As you near your goal, you may find that you are sometimes sabotaging your own success. You may become lazy or apathetic—easily distracted or easily bored. You may find yourself inexplicably doing things that you know are counterproductive to your goals.

This is your old programming trying one last time to keep you from changing. Now is the time for the discipline you've learned as you worked through the process to assert itself. Change your focus from the big picture to the task ahead of you. The big picture is still important—this is just a technique to defeat self sabotage. At this point, each step brings you closer to your goal. Keep your mind on the idea of one step at a time. All your planning brought you to this point, and your journey is laid out clearly in front of you. All you have to do is follow the path that you created for yourself.

If you struggle with the setbacks that occur, remember that times like this are the universe's way of making you stronger. How you deal with challenges defines who you become. Work through the challenges successfully, and you will be more focused on your purpose and your goal than ever before. That increased focus will bring success that much closer.

About Failure

WHAT IS FAILURE? THE definition really depends on who is doing the defining. One person might say it is the inability to accomplish a task. Another person could define it as a part of life. Either one of these definitions would be accurate for that person.

Each of us defines success or failure in our own way. Like most judgments we make about ourselves, our definition can be completely out of line with an objective observation. Most failures are neither as bad nor as permanent as we imagine them to be.

Essentially, failure is the breakdown of a part of a system. On an automobile, brake failure is serious because we depend on the brakes to safely stop the car. A burned-out light bulb, on the other hand, is also classified as a failure because the part of the electrical system that encompasses lights has broken down. With few exceptions, a burned-out light bulb is not as serious a failure as a brake failure.

When we are executing a plan, a failure is when part of a the plan breaks down, resulting in the plan stopping or in a major diversion of tactics in order to accomplish the goal. This definition is the small version of failure—particular to one aspect of a plan. These things happen normally in the course of life and have no reflection on whether the ultimate goal of the plan is achieved or not.

The larger version of failure is when we take the smaller definition and inflate it to mean that the plan, as a whole, is not accomplishable. This definition usually relies entirely on the choice of the person making it. In other words, each of us decides for ourselves if a particular obstacle stops us permanently or if we choose to find another option to make the plan succeed.

If we decide to make the obstacle permanent, then we surrender the options that might otherwise lead to the success of the plan. We accept the fact—whether it is based on information or merely on the opinion of bystanders—that the situation cannot be resolved, and we choose not to find other alternatives.

This acceptance indicates a weakness somewhere in the system other than the individual part that failed. A stronger purpose, a more powerful sense of direction, or a more valid reason for the plan in the first place, may have relegated the smaller breakdown to a temporary obstacle rather than something that caused the breakdown of the entire plan.

In other words, if you let a plan fail, then the "why" was not strong enough. When the cause—the why—is strong enough, we are almost always able to find an acceptable way to overcome adversity. As Gene Kranz determined when rescuing the crew of Apollo 13, sometimes failure is not an option.

The refusal to try again can be rooted in many things. The pain of possible failure may be too great. Again, the "why" is not strong enough. Frustration may render the person incapable of seeing any other alternatives. This may be the willingness of the person to accept failure rather than consider other options. The motivation is not powerful enough to stimulate creativity.

Failure is most often defined by the evaluator—usually someone close to the situation who is not interested or invested in the success of the venture. Naysayers have been around since the beginning of civilization. As has been said before, "Those who say something can't be done are usually interrupted by those who are doing it." If we accept the evaluator's opinion, then we put our happiness and success in the hands of other people.

The question we can ask is, "Is failure permanent?" If you accept the opinion of bystanders, then yes, failure is permanent. But failure is permanent only if, and as long as, we allow it to be. When those who are negative— either about the particular plan or with life in general—affect your happiness and success, then your own success is at risk. To negative people, failure is always permanent.

An objective view would be that there are various types of possible setbacks, all of different degrees, but none of them are permanent unless we let them. Some of the setbacks will require more effort or ingenuity to overcome than others. Many times, the particular setback indicates a path to success that is blocked, requiring a detour that may not have been planned.

Any successful plan will allow for some unforeseen occurrences. Very few plans can be seen all the way through to a successful conclusion from the beginning and anticipate all obstacles. Successful plans don't require such vision. All a good planner needs is to know the desired goal, the resources available, and the steps required to reach the goal. Conditions may change along the way, but part of the reason plans work is the human capability to handle change.

Thomas Edison serves as the standard of handling so-called failure. His story of testing ten thousand elements to find the right one that would work in a light bulb has been repeated many times. When asked about his failures, Edison replied that he had not had any failures. He had instead found ten thousand things that didn't work.

Treasure the information you receive from what doesn't work. Many times these lessons can be applied in other circumstances, giving you an advantage over those who have not faced the situation before. It's called learning from experience not learning from failure.

When you encounter a setback, remember to look at the larger picture. We often get fixated on a particular aspect of the overall plan and forget the bigger goal. General Eisenhower's forces suffered terrible losses when they stormed the beaches of Normandy. If he had become fixed on that one aspect of the battle, he would have seen it as a terrible defeat.

Instead, as every military officer in history who has sent men into combat, he looked at the overall picture and saw that individual skirmishes were lost, but that the overall battle was won. Only by having a map of the entire scenario can a general keep his equanimity and composure. We must have that same type of composure when we evaluate our own plans.

There is only one sure way to avoid failure, and that is never to try anything. If you decide to go check your mail box and the door is locked, you can either unlock it or decide that you are not able to get the mail. Tasks as simple as getting the mail can sometimes lead to overcoming adversity—even if it's only something as simple as a locked door.

However, fear often paralyzes us, causing us to abandon plans altogether. If you have ever told yourself "it probably wouldn't work anyway" or "I couldn't have done it anyway," then you have fallen prey to such a mindset. Those of us frozen by fear are incapable of achieving success unless and until we are able to overcome the fear.

Setbacks are unavoidable in any venture. A plan does not have to be incredibly ambitious to encounter obstacles along the way. As observed above, even something as simple as getting the mail can have obstacles. Creating the proper mindset before embarking on a plan is critical to success.

When you start to execute a plan, think of the reason you want to accomplish it. Give yourself a clear picture of the reason why. After you have imagined the reason behind the plan, tell yourself that obstacles will present themselves. Obstacles are inevitable, but they can be overcome. Go around, go over, go below, or go through the obstacle—there will be options available to make the plan successful.

Steel yourself. It often takes courage to trudge forward when there is no end in sight. The outcome of particular steps of a plan may be unclear, but keep the goal in mind the whole time. This vision of the goal will give you motivation when the plan does not work as smoothly as it could.

Many times we give in to our fear by over planning. "Paralysis by analysis" is common, particularly among those who consider themselves perfectionists. Perfectionism is often the enemy of a successful venture because conditions are never perfect. The planner will spend the entire time trying to figure out what will happen in each particular instance, and it is not humanly possible to calculate all the variables of most human endeavors.

Real courage is having faith even though you know that obstacles and setbacks will present themselves. Having the confidence in yourself, or those carrying out the plan, is vital if you want to get things accomplished. Failure only happens when we lose that courage.

Refuse to give in to failure. Your refusal, by its very nature, will nullify the failure. Winston Churchill exemplified this attitude with a simple quote: "Never, never, never, never give up." Churchill's fortitude helped keep the British nation going during the darkest hours of World War II. He gave British citizens the courage to move forward with their lives.

Sales professionals understand that they work off of percentages. Regardless of the quality of the product they're selling or the nature of the economy they're working in, salespeople will always encounter a certain number of no's during the sales process. The best salespeople know exactly what the percentages are—they may have to speak to three, five, ten, even twenty or more people before they find a prospect who buys their product.

The best salespeople calculate backward from their goal. If they want to make five sales a day and only one out of five people they speak to buy their product, then they know they have to speak to twenty-five people in order to reach their goal. Those people who say no don't represent failure—they are a vital part of reaching the goal. You have to get through all the no's in order to get to the yes's.

Failure only happens to those who allow it to become a permanent part of their world. If you refuse to give in to obstacles, if you always work to find another solution to a problem, if you keep the larger goal in mind, then you will never fail.

Profile: W Mitchell

WHEN HE WAS TWENTY-eight years old, a motorcycle accident nearly killed W Mitchell. His elbow and pelvis were crushed, and the flames from the accident covered three-fourths of his body with third-degree burns. His face was burned beyond recognition. All his fingers and thumbs had been burnt off in the accident, and he was left with two stumps where his hands used to be.

The doctors gave him little chance of recovery. He survived only after numerous operations, including sixteen skin grafts and thirteen transfusions.

Mitchell surprised everyone—six months after his accident, he was back on his feet again and started a successful company.

He also made a name for himself in politics. He ran for Congress despite the fact that his face was grotesquely marked. His slogan was "Send me to Congress, and I won't be just another pretty face."

Mitchell had also earned his pilot's license, and on November 11, 1975, he was prepared to fly to San Francisco on a routine flight—one he had made several times before.

As the plane took off, ice on the wings caused the plane to crash. Mitchell's back was completely crushed, and his spinal cord was irreparably damaged. He would never be able to use his legs again.

Today, despite having no hands and not being able to walk, Mitchell continues to live a full life. He enjoys white water rafting and skydiving. He is a successful businessman and a director of the board to a number of companies.

W Mitchell is in great demand as a motivational speaker because he relates the state of mind that it took for him to overcome his difficulties (from the book *It's Not What Happens to You, Its What You Do About It*).

Points to Remember

Recognize that sometimes things will go wrong.
Don't be caught off guard.

Everyone who has ever tried to accomplish something
worthwhile has suffered setbacks.

The most common reason for a setback is that
you lose your sense of purpose.

Power affirmation: "All things are working together
for my highest good." Know this is true!

Trivial matters can push out the more important
things that you should be doing.

Fear of success stems from old programming
trying to reassert itself.

If you realize that you're off track, become a problem solver.

Prepare for the changes that success will bring.

How you deal with challenges defines who you become.

Write it out. All problems are easier to solve once you
get them out of your head and onto paper.

It's not what you read that makes you successful,
it's what you write.

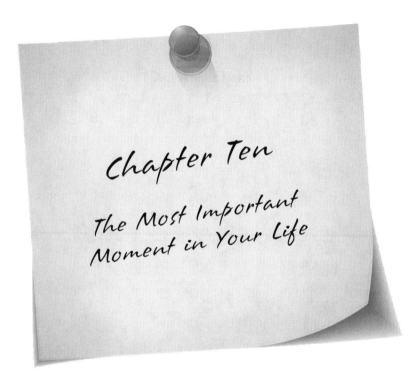

Chapter Ten

The Most Important
Moment in Your Life

—THE MOST IMPORTANT MOMENT IN YOUR LIFE—

> *"Create a definite plan for carrying out your desire and begin at once, whether you are ready or not, to put this plan into action."*
>
> — Napoleon Hill

What's so important about starting right now?

What are the two fundamental steps to success?

What do successful people do?

Is there a way to use momentum to achieve success?

How is motion important to my success?

Hank Stram, an American football coach, says, "Yesterday is a cancelled check. Tomorrow is a promissory note. Only today is cash."

Human beings spend so much of their time looking backward or forward that it takes a special presence of mind to pay attention to now. The saying above paints a vivid picture in a way that hits home. We equate cash to something we can buy things with while the cancelled check and the promissory note are simply pieces of paper.

In the same way, success is possible only through taking action now. The most important moment in your life is the moment that you take action to make your dreams come true. The only moment that you can take that action is right now.

Too many people base their plans on someday, saying, "Someday I'll get a better job," "Someday I'll go on a cruise," or "Someday I'll start saving money." They stagger through life waiting for someday to come and find themselves at the end of their lives wondering what happened.

There are two steps to success, and neither one works without the other. The first step is the creation that happens in the mind in the form of a dream or a fantasy. It's when that moment of inspiration hits, and you realize that something new is possible.

For most people, the process ends there. They dream of a better life and never do anything about it. You can always find these people in a crowd—they're the ones staring out the window, occasionally sighing wistfully. Their dream will never be anything more than a wish.

The second step is action. It's that flurry of activity that makes things happen. Action is great because it's movement, but without the first step of creation in the mind, all it can ever be is simply staying busy. It's like the story of the comedian who told his audience, "I don't have time for laughs, I have a show to do!"

The reason you have to take action now to make your dreams a reality is because there's no such thing in life as a holding pattern. The rest of the world is swirling around you, and if you try to be still, you will be swept away on whatever breeze happens to catch you. Only by having a direction and working toward your goal can you make progress. If you do anything else, your chances of success will decrease. You're either rising or sinking.

Often we will freeze because we're waiting for the right time. Guess what? There's no such thing as the perfect time. It's a myth created by people who were too afraid to do something to be successful.

Successful people don't wait for the right time. They take action now. They understand they will have to make adjustments as conditions change, but those adjustments are much easier when you're in motion and working to improve your situation.

People who wait are always in pain and suffering from the agony of missed opportunities. The right time they were waiting for was the moment that just passed. They live their lives full of regret for actions they should have taken but didn't.

The laws of physics apply to success. Once you're in motion, momentum can carry you farther than you ever imagined. It takes much more energy to get into motion than it does to stay in motion.

By taking action now, you also begin to develop successful habits. Being decisive and action oriented creates routines that help you achieve the success that you desire. It takes time to develop new habits, and the sooner you get started, the sooner the habits can take effect.

It's a law of nature that things take time. The farmer prepares the fields, plants the seed, nurtures the plants, then harvests the crops. There is a season for each of these steps. Even the best farmer can't do all of it in one day— nature won't allow it.

Success also takes time. The laws of nature and of the universe won't let you take shortcuts to achieve success. By taking action now, you can start enjoying your success even sooner.

The season for success is now.

Profile: Gene Kranz

IMAGINE THAT YOU'RE THE flight director responsible for sending a manned spacecraft to the moon and back. The lives of three men are in your hands. Millions of dollars and thousands of man hours of preparation and training have been invested in this mission. Every possible contingency has been examined.

Then the spaceship explodes.

Gene Kranz faced exactly this situation as flight director of the Apollo 13 space mission. Kranz's team was on duty when the service module exploded. Suddenly Kranz's goal was not to land a spacecraft on the moon, but to return the astronauts back to earth safely.

Kranz formed an emergency team whose job was to monitor consumables on the ship so the astronauts could survive the several days it took to return. Then the team had to calculate blasts from the rockets to correct the ship's trajectory so it could safely penetrate Earth's atmosphere.

Finally the team had to calculate power consumption so that there would be enough power left to use the command module to return home.

Kranz had a reputation for being tough and stubborn, but when he saw that the original mission was no longer possible, he adjusted to the higher priority of ensuring the safe return of the astronauts in his care. He and his team had the flexibility to adjust to changing circumstances, and when Kranz had established his new goal, he threw all of his resources at it. He understood that the astronauts aboard Apollo 13 did not have the luxury of waiting. Kranz and his team had to act now.

Most of us won't have goals as monumental and historic as Kranz and his team, but we can use them as an example of working toward a goal and adapting to changes in our environment—establishing a higher-priority goal when necessary and taking action now.

Points to Remember

Success is only possible by taking action now.

Einstein said, "Nothing happens until something moves." So get moving.

Too many people base their plans on someday.

There are two steps to success: the creation that happens in the mind, and taking action.

Successful people don't wait for the right time.

People who wait suffer the agony of missed opportunities.

The season for success is now.

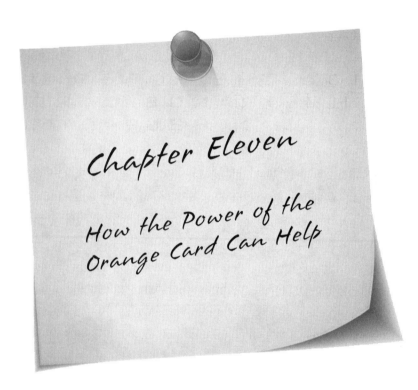

Chapter Eleven

How the Power of the
Orange Card Can Help

–HOW THE POWER OF THE ORANGE CARD CAN HELP–

"Teachers open the door.
You enter by yourself."

— Chinese proverb

How do I access my success?

Why is the Orange Card so special?

How can I augment my use of the Orange Card?

Is there more to this program?

Where do I go next?

The story is told about Frank Lloyd Wright's intricate, architectural masterpiece Fallingwater in Pennsylvania. The home is famous for its cantilevered terraces and its organic connection to nature, especially the waterfall directly below it.

Wright was commissioned by Pittsburgh businessman Edgar Kaufmann to design a vacation home for his family. Months went by, and Wright still hadn't presented the plans to Kaufmann. Finally Kaufman had business to attend to in Milwaukee, just a few hours from Wright's office. Kaufman called Wright and said he'd like to drop by and see how the plans were coming along.

Wright agreed, and with two apprentices standing behind him sharpening pencils, he sat down and went to work. When Kaufman arrived, Wright stood up, walked toward him to shake his hand, and said, "Welcome Edgar, we've been waiting for you."

There on the table were the complete blueprints, with all of the complex architecture required to build such a home. Kaufman left Wright's office impressed with the design. For a home built in 1935, it is still ahead of its time and is now considered a national treasure.

What Kaufman didn't know is that Wright had not written any notes, much less drawn up a blueprint, until three hours before Kaufman's arrival. Wright had carried the entire design in his head, working on it until it was ready to be drawn. When the time was right, he sharpened several pencils and drew the blueprint from memory. If you have ever seen a picture of Fallingwater, you will likely be awed like myself (www.fallingwater.org).

Success for all of us is similar to the story of Fallingwater. We carry the plans around in our heads until it's time to take action.

You have read about the Orange Card and some of its attributes. You wonder what a genuine, Dr. Robson Orange Card really looks like—better yet, what it looks and feels like after you have gone through the process of completing it. You wonder if it can work for you. You might be saying, "He has mentioned the Orange Card many times but I still don't understand exactly what it is and why it is so special." What if you had the special assistance of the man who engineered and designed the phenomenon?

Throughout the book, we've discussed the importance of role models. It's vital that you try to use the image of someone who can provide an example of how the system works. You want a winner to show you how it's done.

With the Orange Card in place in your life, you now can be certain that you have the law of attraction working in your favor. The law of attraction has become incredibly popular with the release of the hit movie *The Secret*. One of the featured speakers in *The Secret* was success expert Bob Proctor.

I am very thankful to be one of a handful of LifeSuccess consultants personally certified by Bob Proctor. What does this mean? It means that not only do I understand the principles of success from personal experience, but I am also able to draw on the vast experience of those before me.

All this is in the effort to help you improve the quality of your life and seriously improve your self-image—the ultimate goal of this book. You will never outgrow your own self-image.

Using the universal laws that have always been at work, you can tap into the frequency that resonates with those things that will truly make you happy. What do you really want when it comes to your love and relationships? What do you really want to see improve in your health? What do you really want to do with your work and career? What position do you really want to be in financially?

The only way any of these things will actually become reality is if you take well-directed action to get your thoughts into a form that will call the universal laws into motion. The Orange Card is the only thing I have ever seen that does this with massive power and incredible simplicity.

The Orange Card is a physical product that you can hold in your hand, and—when created with the proper training—you can summon the infinite powers of magnetism to attract what you have directed to you. It is like the order sheet for what you want, but with qualifications. Many think all they have to do is ask for something and then sit back and wait for it to magically appear. What a joke. The Orange Card addresses this error perfectly.

You can read twenty more books, watch twenty more DVDs, listen to twenty more motivational CDs, attend twenty more seminars, but these will do nothing because they are all passive and not specific to you. You need to have the properly created, worded, and placed Orange Card installed into your life. Then watch as the autopilot setting of your life begins to change.

Yes, I have fashioned several other atomic powered and life changing tools—two of which are so smart, simple, and fun that it would take another book to go into the detail they deserve. I've reserved them for my seminar attendees and my private and corporate clients.

In my three - to seven - hour success trainings, I personally teach and help you create and install these into your life—plus you have a lot of fun doing it.

Your thoughts create your feelings, your feelings determine your actions, your actions determine what you do, and what you do determines your results in every area of your life. So ultimately, your results in life come from your thoughts. The Orange Card is the tool that keeps your thoughts focused on what you want, and, as you have heard many times, what you think about is what comes about.

The Orange Card is more than just a piece of paper. It's the full package available to those who want to learn more. It provides the motivation to start taking charge of your life! The Orange Card takes the dream of success and turns it into reality.

Aircraft are designed to get the most lift with the least resistance. The Orange Card program provides you with that same aerodynamic advantage. Using the Orange Card to aid you with your success gives you the encouragement and information you need and the desire for change that you love.

Profile: Frank Lloyd Wright

Considered the most influential architect of all time, Frank Lloyd Wright designed over one thousand buildings, and more than five hundred of them were actually built. Although well-respected and honored for his architecture now, during his life, Wright had to fight for respect and acceptance.

Born in a rural Wisconsin community, Wright's family struggled financially, and his parents divorced when he was a teenager. His early influences were the musical compositions of Bach and Beethoven and the geometric blocks that he and his mother enjoyed playing with. He entered the University of Wisconsin at the age of fifteen to study engineering. He then moved to Chicago to study and learn the language of architecture. After he graduated, he went to work for a Chicago architectural firm.

To pay his mounting expenses, Wright began to do architectural work on his own. When the owner found out what Wright was doing, he asked him to leave. Wright's so-called "bootlegged" buildings showed his talent for design, and his work began to draw interest from the public.

The first designs were open, low buildings with clean skylines and built with natural materials. Used mainly in single-family homes, these innovative designs reflected the prairie school of architecture.

Over his lifetime, Wright kept refining his theories and ideas about architecture—designing buildings that imitated and worked with nature and the building's natural surroundings.

Wright remained true to his vision through personal and business turmoil that could have derailed him. Arguably the greatest interior space ever designed is his Johnson Wax building in Racine, Wisconsin. Said to be the most impressive house designed in America, with the exception of the White House, is the Fallingwater home mentioned earlier. Wright's Guggenheim Museum in New York represents a pinnacle of showcases for artists worldwide. Take a moment sometime with friends or family to view these on the Internet. It is always inspiring to witness the work of a genius.

How interesting it is to be inspired by man's many creations. Infinitely more phenomenal is the seed of genius that God built into all of us—the power to create, imagine, grow, share, achieve, give, laugh, cry, and love.

Points to Remember

*Frank Lloyd Wright carried his masterpiece
in his head. So do you!*

*The Orange Card is the ultimate and
necessary tool for growth.*

*The Orange Card turns the dream of success into a reality.
It gives you the aerodynamic advantage.*

*The wording on the card is critical and
represents the secret to its power.*

*The Orange Card is a tangible object. Every time
you see and touch it, you instantly activate
the law of attraction.*

The Orange Card is the core of several secret weapons for success.

*The Orange Card is for anyone who really
wants to grow as a person.*

Warning

THE ORANGE CARD HAS THREE RULES
THAT MUST BE OBSERVED

1. It must not violate any of God's laws.

2. It must not interfere with the rights of others.

3. It must be properly created and mathematically sound.

Recommended Resources

SHARPEN YOUR IMAGE!

*E*mma Berryman, Image Consultant trained by the prestigeous London Image Institute, along with Dr. Robson, *The Image Doctor* himself, are focused on making you look your very best!

DID YOU KNOW...
- People make 90% of their judgements about you in the first 3 seconds?
- Your tie is just as important, if not more so, than your resumé during an interview?

REMEMBER...
- You don't get a 2nd chance to make your *1st impression!*
- You're supposed to wear your clothes, they're not supposed to wear you!
- It's easy to maintain your own *personal style* within your new look!
- You attract the people, situations, and things into your life that are in *harmony* with you!

WHEN YOU IMPROVE YOUR IMAGE, YOU WILL...
- Heighten your success in your professional and personal life!
- Enhance your *style*, your *attitude*, and your *life*!
- Get noticed before your clothes do!
- Make the things you want in life *come to you!*

- **Color Analysis:** Learn which colors work best for you and in which situations!

- **Style Analysis:** Figure out what your personal style is!

- **Body and Line Analysis:** Discover what shapes and styles of clothing make you stand out in the crowd!

- **Wardrobe Analysis:** Let's get that closet of yours cleaned out, organized, and working for you again!

- **Personal Shopping:** Are you missing some key pieces in your wardrobe? I'll help you fill in the gaps!

LONDON IMAGE INSTITUTE ®

Tell us what you want — we'll show you how to get it...

winnersedgeconsulting.com • 651.746.9036

WINNERSEDGE CONSULTING

Look Better • Feel Better • Perform Better

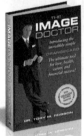

No Smoke, no Mirrors...
no Kidding!

From private parties to corporate functions, **Tyler Erickson** enhances any event with his art and charm. Your guests will talk about their evening long after it has ended!

His combination of physical and psychological manipulation creates **_mind-bending illusions_** that guests will most likely never see again.

Tyler offers a stage act for larger audiences. **_Fast paced_** and with a quick wit, it is centered on audience participation. It is both elegant and unique, and **_he always bonds with the audience, generating fantastic responses!_**

For smaller events and dinner parties, Tyler can perform in a more intimate way, thus allowing the guests to be playfully mesmerized at close-range.

Tyler can perform "**mingling magic**" where he moves through the group, delivering strong and interactive entertainment a few guests at a time.

A Partial List of Tyler's Clients

3M
Regis Corp.
Mopar
Medtronic
Xiotech
Borders Books
General Mills
Champps
Axel's Tavern
Pier 500
Redstone American Grill
Mystic Lake Casinos
Grand Casinos
Eli-Lilly Pharmaceuticals
American Express
Minnegasco
American Guitar
Wells Fargo Banks
Northwest Airlines
Ironworld USA
Blanks USA
Kelly Construction
Litchfield Watercade
Marshall Fields
Banta Catalogue
Hudson Marina
Barnes and Noble

EnviroClean
Graybar Electric
Maximum Potential
DLR Group
Harrison Tile
McCaffery & Associates
Knights of Columbus
Stonearch Productions
Media Loft/Mervyn's

Classes with Tyler

Tyler gives master classes to professional magicians, but also offers introductory classes for beginners. If you are a public speaker, trainer or leader, dress up your presentations with a little magic; let Tyler show you how!

Contact Tyler for Your Event
& About His Newsletter and Classes:

Email: tyler@tylerteach.com
Phone: 612-267-6211
Web General: www.tylererickson.net
Web Classes : www.tylerteach.com

TYLER ERICKSON

Notes

Notes

Notes

Notes

Notes